COMPLIMENTS OF:

## LANCE A. BERGER & ASSOCIATES, LTD.
17 COURTNEY CIRCLE
BRYN MAWR, PA 19010
(610) 525-5332

# Deengineering The Corporation
## Leading Growth from Within

**Lance A. Berger**
**Martin J. Sikora**
**Dorothy R. Berger**

Haverford Business Press
Haverford, Pennsylvania

Published by Haverford Business Press
Post Office Box 507
Haverford, PA 19041

Library of Congress Cataloging-in-Publication Data

Berger, Lance A.
Deengineering the corporation: leading growth from within /
Lance A. Berger, Martin J. Sikora, Dorothy R. Berger
p. cm.
Includes index.
ISBN 0-9662333-0-1
1. Organizational change.   2. Leadership.   I. Sikora, Martin J.
II. Dorothy R.   III. Title

HD58.8.B47 1998                                        LCCN 97-95281
658.4'06--dc20

Jacket cover and text design by Kathe Kisela
Jacket photo licensed from PhotoDisc
Bibliography compiled by Adam S. Berger

Printed in the United States of America

# Contents

# Introduction

This is the case of the wayward ducks. I first became aware of the problem when I visited a division of a large consumer products company located in a pastoral setting in Central New Jersey and noticed something didn't fit. It wasn't the lake in front of the office, nor was it the fifteen ducks swimming in the lake. What finally dawned on me was that I was puzzled by the three dogs lazily snoozing under a grove of trees. The company's human resources vice president cleared up the mystery for me. But more fascinating than his explanation was the labyrinthine exercise that led to the simple employment of dogs to handle the corporate equivalent of an eighth-grade dilemma.

The ducks, its seems, had made the lake a nesting ground where they camped out for several weeks each year. Fine! The company was happy to be a good neighbor, and to welcome the ducks, but was less pleased with what happened when the ducks left the lake and deposited their droppings on the grass. Least happy were the grounds keepers who had to cut the grass. The dilemma: How to confine the ducks to the lake only.

I learned that our consumer products company wasn't the only firm in the area with the problem, so I talked to other companies in quest of a compassionate solution. Sure enough, one of the firms said that it had hired an aviary consulting firm, which had recommended that maintenance people puncture the ducks' eggs, so they would not nest there anymore. This turned out to be a short-term solution. Yes, the ducks were destabilized by their inability to reproduce but they proved resilient enough to lay their eggs at another site, and still return to the original lake. The cost was $100,000, for a complicated solution that ultimately didn't work.

I discovered another company that, with the assistance of a reengineering firm, tried an even more elaborate process for solving the "duck problem." This company tracked migratory birds via radar, and then unleashed a system that emitted predatory bird noises, noxious odors, and ugly liquids to drive the birds away. The cost was $1 million, and it still didn't work. The ever-resilient birds learned to avoid the radar, dodge the sounds, shrug off the liquids and odors, and come back to the lake and the surrounding grass.

The solution to the problem came from a local dog breeder, a low-tech source, who recommended a plan for using the simplicity of nature to outwit the birds. For a minimal monthly fee, the breeder stationed his three hunting dogs at the lake. Each time a duck left the lake, it was chased back by the dogs. With this solution, the ducks have been less adaptable to changing conditions. Now the ducks keep off the grass, the dogs throw a scare into any ducks that stray, and the consumer products company is droppings-free.

Lance A. Berger

---

What is the point of this environmental parable?
Don't let the "solution" get in the way of solving the problem.

# Part One

# Deengineering

———

# 1 Sustaining Growth

The inspiration to write this book comes from our clients, who were continually expressing disappointment and frustration over the inability of their change management initiatives to create and sustain growth. In particular, they were disconcerted by the approach known as "reengineering"– the epitome of the quick fix, and the metaphor for the universal change initiative sought by theory-bound consultants and academics. External studies conducted by The Conference Board, other consulting companies, and our firm confirmed the extent of the problem – that disenchantment was spread far and wide over a huge segment of Corporate America. Much of our consulting work, in fact, turned into damage control to counter the disruptions caused by reengineering-based projects. These experiences led to our first book on the subject, *The Change Management Handbook*.

But there were other disquieting manifestations of the quest for a corporate cure-all. We were influenced and intrigued by the explosive proliferation of business self-help books – to the point where they occupied huge sections of bookstores, libraries, and catalogues, and were expanded to include classroom versions at educational institutions. Books, papers, videos, and slide shows were all either rationalizing the failure of reengineering or, quite significantly, prescribing ways to clean up the destruction wreaked by the reengineering revolution. Reengineering bashing is now commonplace.

Additionally, we were greatly impressed by Eileen Shapiro's *Fad Surfing in the Boardroom*, a remarkable compendium of executive predispositions to grab the latest in-thing as the quick-fix panacea. Placing the whole reengineering movement in a broader perspective, *Fad Surfing* highlights a series of never-ending excuses for not solving problems, or even exacerbating them, because people "blindly sign up for cures without clearly understanding what they can and can't do." In the worst cases, we might add, the cure is chosen without even knowing what the disease is.

Just as sobering is Shapiro's definition of fad surfing: "the practice of riding the crest of the latest management panacea and then paddling out again just in time to ride the next one; always absorbing for managers and lucrative for consultants; frequently disastrous for organizations." A stunning indictment! It says that for many corporate executives, experience is a bad teacher, that change programs often are based more on hope than on smarts, and that the knowledgeable don't know that much. The latest fad technique is grabbed because it's in. And when it fizzles, jump for the next fad, no questions asked. Maybe some day we'll get lucky.

Reengineering, most often the adopted fad, is considered by many to be an old wine in a new bottle. Further complicating managerial change options is the fact that reengineering no longer embodies a single approach but has been generically extended to serve as a metaphor for all over-hyped change management approaches that create inflated expectations of improvement.

When these expectations lead to disenchantment, as is invariably the case, a search for new fads begins, as described by Shapiro. Whether reengineering is offered in its purest form, whatever that may be, or in some diluted variation, virtually all the approaches under its rubric share some common characteristics. Most notably, they all create the illusion that a new combination of business humanism (code word: empowerment) and technological innovation (symbolized by high-speed information systems) can lead people to self-actualization.

However, sterling results have not materialized; managers who decided they needed outside help to meet awesome challenges have been let down. Just as insidious as this string of fad failures is the way managements have been hard-sold on the idea that reengineering would pay off. The source of all wisdom on the supposed efficacy of reengineering is a loose-knit collection of special interests that we call the RAICers – reengineering academic industrial consultants complex. Credit President Eisenhower's phrase – the military-industrial complex – for our brainstorm.

Singly, and at times in partnership, members of the RAIC complex mount highly organized promotions to hawk reengineering, or some other

4

managerial fad, as the universal, all-purpose, easy-to-launch panacea, an off-the-shelf solution for problems so fiendishly complex that they require customized responses. RAICers actually have begun to take over many companies, becoming de facto superiors to the operating executives.

These RAICers have big names, or work for blue-chip consulting firms, thus putting a stamp of legitimacy on their advice and justifying their large fees. Yet, they are using reengineering primarily to promote themselves. Academics, many of whom have never set foot on a shop floor, are selling books on "practical advice." Consultants, fearing their glory days might end, are anxious to create new markets for their services among corporate clients. The typical insider contact is the human resources or information technology professional, who is either seeking more power or, feeling his or her job has been threatened because of poor performance or minuscule value-added contribution, is simply trying to justify his or her position.

The corporate outsider and the former leader removed from the core of power comprise a partnership formed in heaven. It is remarkable how they see eye to eye on cosmetic changes such as following checklists, paying attention to form rather than substance, and emphasizing process instead of results. The "way" represents true "out-of-the-box" thinking – and it can't be wrong if we've done it right!

This is not to indict all academics, executives, and consultants. We have met many who are not wedded to any particular approach, who focus on the business at hand (sustaining growth), and who are not afraid to challenge a suspect fad that is trumpeted as a cure-all. The companies that employ them invariably are first-rate, high-performance organizations, with strong business ethics and great financial achievements. Yet, even these firms have their fad surfers, and anyone reading this book has probably met or locked horns with a RAICer of some type, whether in-house or outside.

Why has reengineering provoked so much disenchantment after beginning with so much promise? Over-hype by the RAICers is one obvious reason. Poor implementation – i.e., someone didn't follow the rules and the checklist – is usually the RAICer's lame excuse. But the principal reason reengineering doesn't cut it is because it is an incomplete, fragmented, slow, and overly complex way of wrestling with a volatile and rapidly changing environment. It is practiced by people operating in functional and insular silos – which, ironically, under the tenets of reengineering, they have pledged to destroy. This tends to leave people going their own ways and failing to communicate or interact just when a harmonized across-the-board effort is needed.

This insularity has additional fallout. Reengineering spends too much time looking inward – in compliance with the checklists – rather than externally at the marketplace, which is usually the wellspring for the power-packed changes that the company really wants to counter. RAICers are focusing on the wrong set of levers, ignoring the market conditions that the company must adjust to in order to restabilize itself and remain a competitive force.

For all its self-promotion as a force of dramatic change, reengineering actually creates a fanciful vision that looks better on paper than it works in the marketplace. Implementation focuses on one or a few elements – for example, organization or operations – eschewing the Total Company Alignment that is needed to keep an organization on a value-adding course. TCA is the proper alignment of strategy, operations, culture, and reward. All four must be in total harmony for the company to grow, remain efficient, stay competitive, and be able to respond optimally to the market-propelled forces of change. What's invariably left after reengineering is a misaligned and shell-shocked company that can barely limp while its marketplace competitors are prospering.

One of the biggest ironies of reengineering is that – although often stressing a reduction in corporate head count – it clings to the shopworn premise that the traditional company-employee relationship survives. It denies the inescapable fact that companies and employees are becoming less dependent on each other, that employment is less secure, that workers' lives are more subject to disruption. Just ask yourself these questions: Can management count on the unswerving loyalty of the workers who survive a reengineering-prompted downsizing? What is their morale like? Do they feel that "they could be next?" Often, the predictable result of reengineering is a change-resistant organization in worse shape than it was when the grand plan was launched.

A really healthy shake-up is more likely to result from a company-led revolution, a complete overhaul in which employees cut through the fog of fads and start to view themselves as individual providers of services in today's highly volatile job markets. This means cutting the umbilical cord between employer and employee, not artificially extending it. It means developing a multiplicity of skills and characteristics that will enhance the worker's "resume value." It means adopting an exit strategy that puts the highest gloss on the employee's value, so he or she will continue to be employed despite the nature of the change. After all, the CEO has an exit strategy – stock options, severance benefits, consulting contracts, board memberships, etc. Why shouldn't the lower-level employee be as well positioned to handle transition?

Developing and refining a solid exit strategy keeps the employee focused on his or her own position, and able to cope with the inevitable changes in the work environment. This helps the employee to adapt to mergers and joint ventures, downsizings and reengineerings, and to take the actions necessary to enhance his or her career growth.

Companies, as well, must accept the concept of personal exit strategies, by doing a better job of identifying and managing the productive employees they really want to keep and instilling the mind-set of change-responsiveness in them. The economic payoff is an established corps of change-responsive workers who can contribute fully to a change initiative from day one – as opposed to wasting precious time and money to train new change leaders who still must prove themselves on the firing line.

This book provides a positive view focusing on sustaining growth. The basis for our definition of deengineering is research and consulting experience. In summary, these findings are:

- Threats to growth are more challenging, numerous, pervasive, and rapid than ever before, and use of the wrong change management methods is alarmingly excessive. This persistent misapplication has created an impenetrable infrastructure of processes, systems, methods, and behaviors that have slowed the organization's responsiveness to change and diverted it from its real purpose – continual strengthening of its ability to compete in the market.

■ The continuing onslaught of change management fads has created credibility problems on a number of fronts, and built change resistance into the work force.

■ The labels of reengineering are enemies of change. They block the creative thinking of truly change-oriented people while prompting in-the-box conformity, internal focus, and the triumph of cosmetic form over substantive results.

■ An organization can handle only a limited number of growth initiatives. Regardless of the number, they must be aligned with each other, and with other key change systems, or none will work.

■ There is a kinder, gentler approach to managing change. It may have the revolutionary title supplied by Tony DeLuca (former Elf Atochem North America Human Resources Senior Vice President), "back to basics."

■ There is so much "fad garbage" in organizations that we must first "deengineer" them, just as a battery must be drained before it is recharged.

■ Most change initiatives actually wind up blocking change instead of facilitating it. Deengineering is simple, flexible, and unfettered. It allows the organization to get down to brass tacks and get on with what must be done to survive. The emphasis is on change, not on the trappings of change.

Former chairman of IBM Corporation, Thomas Watson Jr. said, "It's tougher to keep a business great than it is to build a great business." It is even tougher to keep a business great when the pace of change is so rapid. To keep a company great, it must continually grow. To continually grow, a company must be capable of quickly creating, anticipating, and responding to change more quickly and effectively than its competitors. When the growth process is blocked, a company cannot survive. Growth processes have been stunted by the endless array of fads, like reengineering, which were ostensibly designed to help the growth process but have effectively shut it down.

Our prescription for "keeping a company great" is to use a four-stage process for leading growth from within the organization. These stages are described within the book and are summarized here.

## 1. Taking Back Control of Your Organization

The first step in ensuring that the organization remains on, or returns to, the growth curve requires the careful selection and management of the internal leaders and external advisors who will direct the growth effort. The leaders must then engage in an effort to overcome inertia by eliminating the residue of failed and incomplete change initiatives. Once this is accomplished the firm must establish specific accountability for implementing company-wide growth from top to bottom. A set of eight principles is provided in chapter four to guide the reader through stage one.

## 2. Mastering the Change Management Process

Once change leaders have taken back control of their organization, they need to build a foundation for sustaining growth. This foundation is called the Alignment Blueprint. It is developed and refined on a continual basis through careful implementation of a four-stage change process. The Alignment Blueprint defines nine aligned assumptions which guide the growth process. Sustaining organizational growth is made easier when organizations master this change management process. The four-stage process and the nine Alignment Blueprint assumptions are discussed in chapter five.

### 3. Building the Change-Responsive Organization

After a blueprint is established through the change management process, the organization must institutionalize the resilience required by its Alignment Blueprint. The process of institutionalization is achieved by simultaneously implementing four synchronized processes covering strategy, operations (delivery systems), culture, and rewards. Chapter six presents a set of guidelines describing an alternative approach to creating these processes.

### 4. Building Change-Responsive People

A change-responsive organization is developed when its employees are self-reliant. Self-reliance provides the security necessary for employees to raise their level of risk-taking, which in turn enables them to become active participants in the change process. To be self-reliant, employees must shift their mind-set from being company-employed to being self-employed. Chapter seven explores the relationship between the concept of self-employment and the company's change management process. It also describes the behaviors of change-responsive people and a model for building a personal change plan.

We are less interested in tearing apart the reengineering metaphor and its apostles in the RAIC complex than we are in setting forth a more positive alternative to building change-responsive organizations and people. Our approach involves setting up a conceptual framework that will enable everyone in the organization to create, anticipate, and respond to changes for their products, services, and skills in the volatile markets of the future. But nobody says we can't have some fun at the same time.

So, we urge you to take the "RAIC Self-Assessment Test" to determine whether you are suffering from the RAICer syndrome. We have constructed it by borrowing the favorite tenets of RAICers and one of their pet ploys, the checklist. If you take the RAIC literally, you will see these ideas as model practices; we don't. At the end of the test, we provide scores that correlate inversely to your company's change-responsiveness. The higher your company's score, the more muscle-bound your company is. As you read the test, bear in mind that phraseology and labels may differ. But we think you will be able to recognize the same old stuff and get the point of the exercise.

## The RAIC Self-Assessment Test
(Please answer yes or no to each item.)

1. Your company is a learning organization, or wishes to become one.
2. Your company plans to get to the fourth, the fifth, or perhaps the sixth dimension.
3. Your company has disseminated a self-checklist based on at least five traits of highly successful people or teams.
4. Your company has decided that self-directed (or undirected) teams are the most important organizational units of work activity.
5. Your company has company-wide team-building programs.
6. Team-based pay is being initiated throughout your company.
7. A major broad-banding compensation program has been completed or is underway, to reflect career opportunities within your flattened organization.
8. Your company is exploring the identification of high- and low-impact leaders.
9. Your company wants to use stewards, coaches, and collaborative leaders to replace managers.
10. An important goal of your company is to create a non-hierarchical, de-layered, flat, or horizontal organization.
11. Your company is introducing competency-based pay somewhere in the organization.
12. Your company has a strategy to empower all employees, including a training program to help them empower themselves.
13. Your company believes that employees can define end-to-end solutions.
14. Someone is redesigning one or all parts of your company's value chain.
15. Your company employee values are not migrating in the desired direction.

16. Your company has at least one paradox that must be resolved.

17. Your company's employees regularly check in to share how they are feeling.

18. Your company recently has completed a *group grope;* i.e., people with process (no content) knowledge have gathered in large groups to develop new processes through a process of processes and perhaps help themselves become process owners.

19. Enabling information technology permeates your company through knowledge exchanges.

20. Enabling information has been defined for each of your company's knowledge workers.

21. Your company has a reengineering czar, czarina, emperor, empress, king, or queen.

22. Your company is served by at least one full-time partner from a consulting firm who is exclusively devoted to your account.

23. Your company has been assigned a full-time clipboard-carrying team of junior consultants with a checklist for radical reengineering or business transformation. At least three must be assigned for each internal project, or serve as your internal project team, to comply with the cardinal tenets of reengineering.

24. The consulting firm that helped your company redefine its processes has referred it to another firm for software design, which in turn has referred your company to another firm for hardware, after charging large fees for creating and supporting process redesign teams.

25. Your company's systems integration firm doesn't know your business strategy.

26. Someone in your company knows and has worked with exogenous variables.

27. Your company has employed a prominent academician (or used his or her book) who has never managed a P&L statement, closed a factory, hired, fired, or trained an employee.

28. Your company employs one or more people who call themselves organization development professionals.

29. Your organization motivates its employees to engage in fundamental thinking, out-of-the-box thinking, alternative thinking, radical thinking, or group consensus thinking.
30. Your company uses the Pareto Principle to manage throughout the organization.
31. Your company is actively engaged in knocking out its silos.
32. Your company is committed to the virtual organization, virtual teams, virtual anything.
33. In your company, jobs have been abolished and replaced by roles.
34. Your company favors a triangle, diamond, or circle as a conceptual framework to explain your business situation.
35. Your company uses 360-degree performance appraisals, or at least 270-degree performance appraisals.
36. Your company has engraved its mission and vision statements on plastic to carry in wallets, install in elevators, and place on desks.
37. Your company has merged strategic thinking and strategic planning.
38. Your company promotes loyalty-based management.
39. Many of your company's employees are involved in either stress management or conflict resolution training programs.
40. Organization charts have been eliminated from your company's documentation.
41. Your company emphasizes consensual decision making.
42. Your company has developed core competencies for technology transfer.
43. Your company is engaged in extensive benchmarking activities for all parts of the value chain and its supporting functions.
44. Despite your customer-oriented work force, your company's customers have no more brand loyalty than before.
45. Your company's senior executives believe they can radically transform the organization through reengineering.
46. Your company has circulated an article reporting the positive impact on stock prices of the perceived value of reengineering, value chain improvements, outsourcing, or the competitiveness of human resources processes.

47. Your company's head-hunting firm has positioned itself as an executive search and business consulting organization.
48. Your company has purchased three or more different types of software packages to do process mapping.
49. Your company is fascinated by "as if" flow charts.
50. Your company believes the "reengineering revolution" has gone only halfway and you would like to see Michael Hammer take it all the way.

Give your company one point for each "yes" answer and rate your RAIC quotient in accordance with the following scale:

| Score | Interpretation |
| --- | --- |
| 50 | Your company is paralyzed and is operating in a massive zone of self-deception; crisis is massive and people do not have time to work on the business problems; RAICers are ecstatic, but the Titanic is sinking. |
| 35 - 49 | Competitors are eating your company's lunch, but your company is still convinced it has most of the answers. Someone will most likely buy your company, which makes RAICers very happy – until they figure out they will be the first to go when the sale is completed. |
| 25 - 34 | Your company is still competitive in the short term. Your company's employees are largely spending time on business-related activities. RAICers are not comfortable because not enough time is being spent redesigning processes and introducing new enabling technology, and employees are not empowered to redesign themselves out of their own jobs yet. |

0 - 24      Your company is largely devoting its time to dealing with its markets and products. The company's focus is on results, and it is getting results. RAICers are either nonexistent or very unhappy with the lack of new management programs.

Now that you have taken the RAIC test, enjoy the balance of the book. As you read chapter two, see how many of the fifty items on the checklist apply to the WhiteChips case.

# 2
# The Reengineering Game

It was a beautiful Monday morning in Silicon Valley, but Jack White was in a foul mood. That was rare – not the gorgeous morning, but Jack's disposition. Normally the most even-tempered of men, the CEO of WhiteChips, the much-admired leader in the computer chip industry, seldom had a reason to scowl. WhiteChips was the embodiment of corporate Eden, with twenty-two years of increasing sales and earnings, generous margins, rising stock prices (which produced the industry's highest P/E multiple), expanding returns to shareholders, and a ceaseless stream of technological breakthroughs and sparkling new products. Jack basked personally in the success of his creation, gaining great wealth, yearly mentions as one of America's most able CEOs. "More damn money than I'll ever know what to do with," he often said.

So what could possibly make Jack so sore? He had spent the weekend reading and re-reading the reports from his key managers on the latest generation of chips. They added up to what Jack considered a crisis. He did not like crises – he was not used to them, unless they developed in his beloved R&D laboratories. But those were just technical challenges that could easily be overcome by great minds working together. "We don't need any big egos around here," was Jack's motto, and despite his own fame and the adoration of his peers, he liked to keep as low a profile as possible, and to refer to himself as nothing more than a captain who couldn't make it without a good crew.

To understand why Jack was so uptight, we have to understand the strategy and culture that he had inculcated into WhiteChips. From the time he created the company, WhiteChips was driven by Jack's obsession with technological supremacy. The industry was in such a constant state of change, he argued, that giving up the lead at any time was a sure pathway to disaster. Moreover, the engineer-turned-CEO harbored an almost pathological fear of being overtaken and having his products become obsolete overnight. If a bit extreme, Jack's mind-set became the driving force behind WhiteChips' seemingly effortless attainment of both rapid growth and solid market leadership. WhiteChips bet heavily on a continual flow of new and innovative products from the company's laboratories, speeding them to market well ahead of competitors, enjoying a big edge for as long as possible, and then moving on to the next generation, even if the older products had to be cannibalized. And the strategy worked, because Jack himself was continually in the labs working side by side with his top technical brains.

While Jack appreciated the other arms of WhiteChips, it was clear that the technical hands were his corporate elite. After all, Jack reasoned, if we turn out superior chips, manufacturing them and selling them to our customers should be a piece of cake. Jack watched the sales figures largely to make sure that customers were accepting his latest baby, and he kept the sales and production people happy by paying them well. But to him the scientists were the backbone of the company.

Yet, this dichotomy was never visible to outsiders, even the financial analysts who covered WhiteChips like a blanket and fawned over Jack at the annual bashes the company threw for them at a posh hotel. Who cared when the results were so glittering? So nimble, so agile did WhiteChips appear to the world at large that it was considered the embodiment of great change management. Not only had WhiteChips been the primary trigger of change in its market, but it had also swiftly adapted to whatever alterations were required in its operating mode. Change creates crisis, and constant change creates constant crisis, and WhiteChips had created crisis for its competitors, while it sailed blissfully through the eye of the storm.

This time around it wasn't so easy, however. The latest generation of chips, the company's hefty bet on its future, was taking longer to develop than expected, and certainly longer than prior generations had taken. The delays were not very serious, but they upset the whole timetable. This was a new and disquieting experience for WhiteChips, which always opened the window of opportunity, rather than wait for someone or something else to open it. If the problems were not ironed out quickly, the delays could cascade and cost WhiteChips much of its market edge.

To enhance its superiority in the form of increased power and greater user-friendliness, the latest generation was based on a new material that was unfamiliar to WhiteChips' scientists. They had the smarts to learn the ropes fairly quickly, but until they did, some delay was being built into the process.

Jack could understand the developmental problems, but he was less patient with other concerns, such as manufacturing and selling. Manufacturing had never been a great problem in launching previous generations, or at least that's the way it seemed to Jack. Rather than revise the production process entirely, the company had been able to accommodate each new generation with a modicum of line alterations. In fact, the manufacturing group was always muttering about how "we have to break our nuts to get ready for a new generation and nobody upstairs really appreciates it." Nevertheless, even the greater changes required this time around wouldn't take all that long. But when combined with the delays in the laboratory, the production slowdown meant a hold in the introduction timetable which WhiteChips was not used to.

The sales force was another source of potential trouble. Jack had always taken the position that his chips sold themselves, that the salespeople simply acquainted customers with the new products and booked the orders. In fact, the salespeople were increasingly being called on to show clearly why it was worth the customers' while to buy the new chips, retool their operations, and make product changes to adapt to the new chips. Plus, the salespeople needed time to familiarize themselves with the selling points of the new chips, and a rough idea of when they would have something tangible to show their customers.

But the worst was yet to come – the real source of Jack's funk was that, after the increased cost of the new materials, the development, and the changes in the production line, the new generation simply would not return the profit margins that WhiteChips had traditionally enjoyed. Although not a financial wizard, Jack quickly calculated a triple whammy from the margin squeeze. If WhiteChips raised its prices to widen the margins, customers in the price-sensitive market might balk, no matter how superior the new chips were. Yet, holding the price line to buoy sales would shrink profit growth and drag the stock price – which was an not inconsiderable concern to Jack, whose vast wealth was based on a 53% ownership of WhiteChips stock. Perhaps most critical of all, the narrower margins threatened WhiteChips' true ace in the hole, the source of the substantial amounts of cash needed to fund the development of future generations of chips.

Jack's mood hadn't mellowed by the regular Monday morning staff meeting, and it was contagious. The management team, normally infused with Jack's good humor and a continuing series of glowing reports from around the table, grew somber and morose, hardly the best environment for tackling a critical decision.

Finally, Bob Rogers, the CFO – and a Harvard MBA – spoke up, although it was obvious that methodical Bob had been planning his pitch for some time, and timing it perfectly. "There's only one way out," Bob started. "This is bigger than any of us. Maybe we're a little bit spoiled, but the fact is that we've never had to face this many problems at one time. It's like a seesaw. If we tip toward one side, the other goes up in the air. I read about techno value chaining by the Chammer brothers in their latest book. *The Wall Street Journal* and the *Harvard Business Review* say it's catching on. We need to balance things off, and to do that, we'll have to bring in someone from the outside to take a fresh look at the whole deal, perhaps even techno value chaining, and give us an objective recommendation on how to tackle everything at one time. When it comes right down to it, each of us has his or her own axe to grind, no matter how much we don't like to admit it." "I'll be honest with you," Jack replied. "I find it hard to believe anyone knows the market or the company as well as we do." "Quite frankly Jack, that sounds like a 'not invented here' attitude," Bob shot back. "I'm not saying a consultant will know as much as we do, but we're so close to everything that maybe we've been blinded to the real problems and need some outside advice."

"Well," Jack replied, still skeptical, "that may be the case, but this person had better be good. Do you have someone in mind?" "You bet," Bob shot back. "My old classmate, Jim Clay, is a principal at MBK&H. He heads its high-tech consulting practice, and he knows the market really well. In fact, his undergraduate degree is in engineering. He's real solid and has a great track record in working with all kinds of high-tech clients. He really understands our unique problems, and the company is ready to partner with us. It also has a great methodology. It was developed by several professors who devoted their entire sabbaticals to creating indices and benchmarks to support attaining our vision." "Where has Jim done this before?" Jack queried. "In several places, but because of the length of the projects we can't tell the level of success. But the CEOs tell us the boards are off their backs."

"And how much is all this wonderful help going to cost us?" "Only a half-mil," Bob replied. "I'm the last guy in the world to shell out money for anything, but this is a reasonable fee for what we will be getting. Jim will get to the bottom of this in a hurry, and our returns will be terrific."

Within three months, Jim was back with his report. If Jack and company were pleasantly surprised by his speed, the recommendations didn't go over all that well. They were indeed shockers.

"Now, there's not much I can help you with on the development side," Jim led off, striking a simpatico note with Jack. "My research shows that you are leagues ahead of your competitors technologically. Of course, I had done a good bit of research on a generic basis and my follow-up research only confirmed my original conclusions. While you may be having some trouble getting the new materials to work for you, your competitors aren't even in the first stages of using them. So, even with your hold-ups, you are still in the driver's seat there."

Jack beamed. He was cocked and primed for the not-so-hot news ahead. "The market is another story," Jim continued. "It still is highly price-sensitive, as you already know, and as good as your new chip may be, it is going to meet some resistance from customers if they perceive that the price is out of proportion to the added value it delivers. So, there's got to be a balancing act between the prices and your costs, to keep margins steady. Again, that's coals to Newcastle as far as you're concerned."

"So when we get back down to it, the real problem is the margin squeeze. How do we lick that? You will have to totally reengineer the company – a radical change of course. Frankly, I don't know of many companies, no matter how successful they are, that won't say they haven't done reengineering after operating for twenty-two years in the same format. The changes are too great to just stand pat. You've been lucky because for the most part you've created the changes in the market, but now they are catching up with you."

Jack, the consummate engineer, was stumped by the prospect of reengineering a company. Most of his team, technical or otherwise, didn't know from beans about it either – that's why they brought in Jim. And they had been softened up for the punch line. After deftly deflecting a few questions on reengineering, Jim was ready to move in for the kill.

"Reengineering means shaking up the company to make it better attuned to the marketplace and current conditions," Jim continued. "First, the sales force. You've got too many salespeople, given your situation. It's not that the number is particularly out of line with your size or your business, but my research finds that your chips actually sell themselves. You set the industry standard, and your reputation is such that your customers actually await the new generations. So, you don't need as many salespeople, and it's a key area where you can cut costs. By the way, your salespeople are the highest paid in the industry, so the savings will be significant."

"But worst of all is your customer service function. It's slow to respond to customer needs, and is not hooked into an information system that will modulate the correct availability of products to demand. By the way, we should knock down all the functional silos as a by-product of more rigid walls between your groups. This blocks communications and, worse yet, inhibits the creation of teams. But let's forget about this now and focus on the sales force."

Mark Rosenthal, the sales VP, knew from experience that new generations were often a tough sell, and wasn't buying it: "How do you square what you said about price sensitivity with what you just said about the chips selling themselves? It seems to me that we need living, breathing, red-blooded salespeople out there letting the customers know why it pays them to buy our chips."

Although caught off guard, Jim didn't show it. "I'm not saying you don't have to do any selling. I'm saying that once the customer is softened up, there's no need to continue to stroke him. In fact, once you get the new chips in, your salespeople can be freed up to go after new customers. You simply don't need this many salespeople."

That analysis was right off the top of Jim's head, and Mark spotted it as an ad lib from the first word. Mark – who started as a WhiteChips sales-man, and liked to be in the field with customers as much as Jack liked to be in the labs – knew from experience that Jim was off-base, but he seemed to be alone. Mark was the lone voice crying foul in a sea of technical types, like Jack, and penny-pinchers, like Bob. Mark started to protest, but Jack, who never fully appreciated how his salespeople got his latest creations to market, cut him off. "Let Jim finish. We'll have plenty of time to kick this around later."

"Now, when you reduce the sales force you can also cut back the num-ber of support people," Jim resumed. "So, you take out a whole layer of sales administration and other costs, and the savings won't stop there." Mark, a firm believer in having salespeople sell and having their papers pushed by paper-pushers, was close to an explosion, which he managed to stifle, knowing that he wasn't going to get anywhere, given Jack's state of mind.

"Frankly," Jim chimed in, "I'm a bit appalled at the way you empha-size the sales and the other functions without consideration for a balanced scorecard approach. For a company in the computer business, your infor-mation systems are in the Dark Ages. The production systems for handling orders and shipping need a good shake-up. One of your customers can do it at a low cost and you'll be making brownie points with it. So, you've got systems replacing some of the salespeople. You can not only cut costs but implement a just-in-time delivery system."

Mark was seething even more. He had practiced just-in-time delivery long before it had a name. Had Jim bothered to check whether there was any dissatisfaction with customers over delivery timetables? Mark had done it constantly and never found any problems. And as for new systems, Mark long had been pressing Bob for money to do some upgrading, and Bob had always said no.

Jim then turned his attention to production. "You've got one plant too many," he said. This floored manufacturing VP Hank Messina, a hard-nosed industrial engineer who constantly watched costs and productivity at the company's three plants, and who was recognized around the industry as a master of efficiency in high-tech production.

"You can get the same production out of your plants here and in Illinois as you can by operating all three plants. Close the one in Texas. That will cut your work force by 300 people down there alone, as well as some additional support people and middle managers. I know it's an efficient operation, but that means you can sell it for a nice amount of cash. If you concentrate on the production here and in Illinois, you will be able to make the line modifications easier, run a tighter ship all around with your production runs, and really concentrate on total quality management. And we need to get you on a nine sigma-0 defect program."

Hank, whose chips had the lowest fault tolerance level in the industry, was as astounded as Mark had been, but seeing how his sales compatriot had fared, he wasn't about to raise a fuss now.

Jack's first assessment was that the plan was made in heaven and that it solved a lot of problems simultaneously. But before buying into it, he wanted to be certain that Jim was right about Jack's primary interest, that WhiteChips was indeed technologically far ahead in the marketplace.

"Well, we have good input on that," Jim replied. "But just to make sure, we checked it out with Prof. Kundleman at the university. He's number one in academia on computer chips, and I know you have used him." A respected academic could let the client know the consultant was providing an objective viewpoint, that did not favor any single function.

"It was all very confidential. No hint we were working with WhiteChips. Prof. Kundleman says you've still got the whip hand and everybody else hasn't even entered the home stretch."

From that point on, Jim had made a sale, not only gaining acceptance of the report but also an additional fee for masterminding the actual reengineering project. Jack, whose technical questions had been answered, had bought in. Bob, savoring a huge reduction in costs, was in Jim's camp. Mark and Hank and some of the others were still fuming, but they knew it would be politically correct to start showing some team behavior. And while the report would be debated vigorously for weeks after that, the die was cast on that first Monday.

Although Jim was home free, he still had more to suggest. "Listen," he pointed out, "reengineering involves more than just moving people around, downsizing, cutting costs, and the like. It's more radical. Today, radical means competitive. You've really got to show you're committed to this thing from top to bottom, to get the message out to your people."

Jack was beginning to get a bit uneasy at this point. The meeting was dragging on and he was anxious to get back to the labs. He retorted, "What are you talking about? What stronger message can we send than closing a plant, chopping the sales force, and cutting another big group? It's the visible signal of change we've been searching for. You know we've never done anything like that before. In fact, we've always been strong on keeping the head count down. Analysts tell us we've got the highest sales per employee among our peer companies. I know we have to do something different to get our problem under control, but I really have to worry about the morale of the survivors when they see their friends being fired."

"Precisely," Jim responded. "I am thinking very much of the morale problem. You've really got to do something that endures and makes the point that this reengineering was needed. I know that this is something foreign to you folks, because you've been decentralized and unstructured, but believe me, it's that extra touch that makes reengineering succeed."

"Okay, let's have it already," sputtered Jack, who at this stage was willing to buy anything to get out of there.

"Well, you've got to have the right artifacts that symbolize change, and that means changing your lingo. Let me explain. Descriptions of your facilities, like laboratory, library, executive offices, and the like, are old hat. They don't really reflect their roles in the reengineered organization. So, they have to be changed."

Jim read off his list of new nomenclature:

Library – Corporate Learning Center

Laboratory – Technical Resource Center

CEO's Office – Executive Team

CFO's Office – Fiscal Responsibility Center

Employees – Associates

Barbara Gorman, the human resources vice president, was the dissenter this time. She had always taken the position that her job consisted of getting the operating people the talents they needed posthaste; allowing the operating managers to set pay based on the worth of their workers; keeping the right records; and making sure the company was in line with all employment and labor laws and regulations. Now she was hopping mad. She knew that rather than accept the pompous labels as symbols of beneficial change, the work force would regard the new lingo as a crock, and that mere words wouldn't do a thing to ameliorate hard feelings and low morale. If anything, they would aggravate the backlash that she already knew would require special efforts from her office to contain. Besides, changing the signs and the company literature would take a big part of her budget at a time when she needed every cent to handle the fallout from the reengineering. But Barbara fared no better than Mark and Hank. Her objections were quickly brushed aside.

So, the games began. The plant in Texas was quickly closed and sold for more than $90 million, half of which was used to repurchase stock and the remainder redeployed into R&D. The work force was chopped by more than 500 people, an incredible 20% reduction in head count. Cost reductions immediately found their way to the bottom line. The reengineering linguistics were pushed with gusto. All the first-level supervisors were knocked out, and through the magic of self-directed teams, the manager-to-staff ratio dropped to 1 manager/250 staff. A new team-based compensation system was installed to help everyone share in the gains of productivity and the total number of salary grades was reduced from

20 to 4. This "broadbanding" created euphoria because no one could be demoted anymore, and many believed that salary increases were unlimited. Stock analysts rejoiced – at least for a few months.

While Jack and his scientists continued to struggle with the new chip, three competitors brought out new generations that improved on WhiteChips' existing model while still using conventional materials. WhiteChip's leadership position was suddenly shaken. When WhiteChips finally entered its great advance into the field, it faltered because of bad timing. Customers were doing just fine with competitors' chips, and were unwilling to change.

Although WhiteChips eventually recovered, it was never the same; its myth of invincibility had been shattered. It had let down its customers, suppliers, investors, and employees. Adding insult to injury, the reengineering consultant couldn't install the remaining $20 million of hardware and software needed to upgrade the plants and customer services. When it came to delivery of a practical asset, WhiteChips had to hire another consulting firm.

# 3 The Failure of the Reengineering Game

How did WhiteChips fall from its dominant position so quickly? How did it go from king of the hill to low man on the totem pole almost overnight? WhiteChips had never before been hit by a change trigger – a force that threatens to destabilize a company, while simultaneously posing threats and opportunities – instead, it had been the perpetrator of change triggers on its competition through its technological prowess. Faced with an external change trigger, it was unable to cope.

Furthermore, WhiteChips ceded control over what it knew best to outsiders in the Reengineering Academic Industrial Consulting Complex (RAIC), the false prophets of symbolic change rather than real change. It had been bitten by the virus of radical restructuring, which was total overkill considering WhiteChips' problems. In the end, reengineering solved none of the company's problems, aggravated many of them, and even created new ones.

Of course, the reengineering executed under Jim Clay's tutelage meant change. But for what purpose and to what effect? Reengineering changed the outward trappings but did not get at the root causes of WhiteChips' problems. Nor did it mobilize WhiteChips toward aligning its key functions for growth.

Deengineering is keeping control of organizational change, rather than farming it out to RAICers with off-the-shelf solutions. It's making sure that all parts of the organization are meshing, during times of change as well as of stability. It's listening to the market and keeping in step with it. It's coping with change on an ongoing basis, accepting that change is a crisis that is here to stay, rather than indulging in "fad surfing."

With Jim Clay's expensive help, WhiteChips took all the wrong steps in trying to find a solution to the margin squeeze. It opted to bite a bullet that didn't exist, and to suppress its own problem solving skills in favor of a messenger from on high.

In this chapter, we will review where WhiteChips misfired, with the aim of showing how getting back on track could have been more effectively accomplished under deengineering. However, WhiteChips had long been a corporate disaster waiting to explode. It did not suddenly get into a bind because of a margin squeeze and technical problems with the new product line – it had been headed that way for years. Despite its image and self-description as the epitome of the change-responsive organization, WhiteChips was anything but. It could handle change only as long as it was driving the chariot, and creating crises for others. While creating crisis is desirable, WhiteChips also needed to manage change when the triggers of change were being squeezed by someone else. Its inability to respond to external forces left WhiteChips vulnerable to a smooth-talking RAIC pitchman. In the next chapter we will describe the change-responsive organization from top to bottom, and point to the holes in WhiteChips' organization. The reengineering-based mistakes in launching the new chip lines are quite overt, but the entrenched organizational problems behind the mistakes are more subtle.

For example, WhiteChips' first mistake was underestimating its ability to solve its own problems in-house. When confronted with a brand-new kind of problem – the margin squeeze – it took its inability to come up with an instant solution as an inferiority complex. It went from a firm belief in its own mystique as a quick-fix problem solver, into a managerial funk in which its decisionmaking machinery was virtually paralyzed. It was ready not only to believe the messenger but to crown him king. Introducing a new product line with advanced materials, at margins commensurate with historical performance, indeed comprised a highly complex problem. It was one that needed more time to be dealt with – an overnight solution was impossible. Moreover, its very complexity indicated that it was a problem that needed special attention and custom-tailored solutions. Who better to deal with it than WhiteChips' own people? And who worse than an outsider with a generic approach? But WhiteChips, formed in Jack White's mold, was an impatient organization, with a history of sometimes moving products to market too speedily.

Ironically, this impatience did not permeate all elements of the company. If Jack White and the scientists didn't know it, certainly the sales and manufacturing people knew of the real-world problems that exploded every time a new line was brought forth. The problem was that those issues were rarely factored into the overall decisionmaking machinery, which had Jack at the controls. That was evident from the meeting at which Jim Clay's report was received. WhiteChips' research and development, sales, and manufacturing functions were misaligned. The company's survival was threatened and no one recognized it.

What Jack White refused to appreciate was that Mark Rosenthal's and Hank Messina's attention to details had not only been instrumental in the repeated success of sequential new lines but that the new product introductions had been executed in a way that made the whole process look seamless. Even Jim Clay was taken in by the illusion, although not unwillingly, because it fit perfectly with what he wanted to tell Jack.

Hank's manufacturing operation was one of the principal reasons that WhiteChips enjoyed such high margins. He and his top aides repeatedly kept atop the R&D effort, to give themselves sufficient lead time to set up their lines for the newest chip generations. They worked on maintaining and acquiring needed equipment, removing bottlenecks, keeping production crews at optimum levels, and getting the product into the distribution pipeline in a timely fashion. Furthermore, they had done this with three plants, the minimum level that Hank felt was feasible. Certainly, no one else in the company had objected to the number before, and there was no indication that the firm was overmanned.

Just when Hank was wrestling with the problem of getting his lines to handle chips with new materials, he was told he must drop one of his plants. This meant revamping the California and Illinois plants to handle increased production, which exacerbated his troubles and expanded his work load.

Trying to resolve all these problems at the same time turned out to be almost impossible. When the chips were finally ready for production, Hank's lines were far from ready to handle them. Manufacturing delays slowed the introduction and allowed competitors to plug the innovation gap at the market's leading edge. Whatever savings were realized from selling the Texas plant were given back by the manufacturing snags.

A not dissimilar situation brought the sales force to its knees. Like Hank, Mark had tried to argue that merely foisting a new generation of chips on the market wasn't going to work. His salespeople, he reminded fellow managers, had to sell their guts out to get customers to buy the new lines – and this time, the sales effort would be even more complicated. Because of the new materials, the changes that customers would have to make were more complicated than ever. WhiteChips' salespeople would have to ratchet their skills and long relationships with customers up to extraordinary levels, to make them accept the pricey new chips, superior though they might be.

Instead, what did Mark face? – a shrunken crew. At a time when he most needed his experienced salespeople, reengineering reduced his force and dampened morale. Out went many of his best people. The remaining people, grossly unmotivated, didn't trust management. Coverage of the market was poor, and customers were not being called on – but, true to the reengineering code, sales teams were regularly meeting to plan customer calls, do 360-degree appraisals, and develop their own incentive programs.

Of course, neither Mark nor Hank actually had to lay off many people themselves. They didn't get the chance. As soon as wind of the reengineering blew through WhiteChips, prized salespeople and manufacturing experts were on their way out of the swinging doors – most of them to jobs with elated competitors. Instead of mobilizing the work force around a carefully planned set of company growth options, the company created both organizational and personal confusion. Not only did the work force feel that its authority and its right to make decisions had been usurped, it also believed that it could come up with better solutions if given the opportunity – it was the worst of both worlds. The most marketable and creative people left and morale dropped, the reverse of what the consultant had promised. Jim had encouraged management to force people to join reengineering teams that would plan how to increase speed and eliminate non-value-creating activities. Turnover would cease and no new people would be required, because everyone would be involved – everyone would be empowered by the CEO. Instead, it was a monumental backfire!

Finally, those wonderful exercises in nomenclature – the Learning Centers, and so on – did about as much good as a stampede of wild elephants. The initial reaction was snickering; Barbara had warned that the new labels would be treated by the action-oriented employees as something out of Alice in Wonderland. But even she underestimated their effect. After a time, the pomposity of the new names wore on employees' nerves, and became the object of much anger, since they symbolized the reengineering program that had turned WhiteChips from a sleek greyhound into a lethargic old mutt. And, instead of having a free hand to deal directly with the morale problems, Barbara was ordered, over her protests, to concentrate on changing signs and rewriting company literature.

In this way, three key players in the corporate change effort were diverted from the company's real needs to the dubious priorities of reengineering. How many people under them were similarly thrown off-course? Enough to throw all of WhiteChips out of sync.

Ironically, Mark, Hank, and Barbara had warned of the consequences, but Jack White had refused to listen. This was partially because of his own unshakeable prejudices, and partially because they had been shrewdly exploited by Jim Clay. It did not take a rocket scientist to figure out where Jack was coming from. All Jim needed was the right interpretation of the information; he could easily discern that Jack's heart was in the laboratory, that deep down everything else in the company was secondary – and he structured his report accordingly. Oddly, no mention of an exit strategy was contained in Jim's report – further putting WhiteChips at risk if the plan failed.

Manufacturing wasn't that big of a deal to Jack. Hence, one plant could be jettisoned, and not only produce big savings but a huge cash influx as well. Salespeople were virtually irrelevant to him, because he believed that the product literally sold itself. And the organization hadn't been tinkered with in twenty-two years. Surely, it was time to do something about that

31

because, after all, the world outside had changed, and peer companies were going the same way. Jack, who always thought of organizational charts as superfluous, felt that since he liked the rest of what Jim said, he might as well go along with the charts as well. After all, what difference did it all make?

Jim pulled out every stop to make sure Jack heard what he liked. He emphasized the great quality of the product and its automatic acceptance by customers. His reference to the academic expert, Prof. Kundleman, was right out of *The Hidden Persuaders*. Jim had played right to Jack's prejudices, confirming that WhiteChips was ahead of the pack technologically because an impartial, widely respected outsider had said so. And given Jack's technological bent, it was not accidental that Jim chose a technical point, the MIS, to demonstrate where improvements could be made on the sales and manufacturing sides.

The nagging problem of the margin squeeze still existed. Deengineering could not necessarily have solved the problem overnight. But reengineering, at least in the format espoused by Jim Clay, was definitely the wrong way to go – a distraction, and at best a temporary palliative in the guise of true change. If nothing else, deengineering – keeping it simple and letting the on-scene pros handle the job – would have brought into sharp focus the fact that conditions were not as bad as Jim had portrayed them, and that the supposed benefits of reengineering would be negated by stark trade-offs.

Insiders would have known the problems of the new chip lines first-hand, and would have been able to surmise how their personnel would react to changes that had little correlation to the market. How would they have dealt with the margin squeeze?

Let us start by recapping Jim Clay's solution, a series of quick fixes that focused on one area – costs. It is true that the huge cut in costs immediately widened margins and fattened the bottom line. But what do you do for an encore? Was a temporary boost in margins a fair price to pay for the loss of key talent, the rupture of long-standing client relationships, the loss of market leadership, and the failure of the introduction of the latest chip line?

In short, Jim Clay offered a temporary solution with little value for the long haul. Following the tenets of deengineering, insiders would have started by asking how the squeeze had originated. Were margins so much lower than before that action as drastic as throwing the baby out with the bathwater was necessary? Wasn't some margin squeeze inevitable when introducing an ice-breaking chip? Or was Jack panicking simply because the margin just wasn't what it had been? WhiteChips insiders may not have liked the margin squeeze any more than Jack, but they may have concluded that it was something the company would have to live with for a while – an inevitable function of expanding a fast-moving market, where complexity increases with each new generation.

Under deengineering, change-oriented insiders direct the change process, and advisors are used simply to supplement the in-house expertise. Insiders who were accountable for results would know if a temporary sacrifice of price and margin were necessary to stay ahead of the competition. Given their skills at manufacturing and selling, it is likely that they would have generated sufficient productivity and revenues to regain historic margins before long. (The temporary lapse would be skillfully explained to investors as the price of progress.) Ultimately, insiders would have fashioned a program that would have kept the company viable over the long run. It might have included some hybrid reengineering aspects, as well as other initiatives – such as acquisition, or the use of savvy outside experts who could bring practical approaches to the table. Equally important is that encouraging proven company change leaders to create initiatives would have sustained WhiteChips during the difficult period when it was trying to rationalize its new line. These people would not have been beaten to a new generation by competitors. They would have seen that the squeeze was a temporary setback. The change leaders would have acted as positive role models for less change-oriented employees – teamwork in its truest sense!

Why? Only WhiteChips was in a position to bring out the vastly improved chips with the advanced materials. No matter how good the competitors' new products were their edge would have been of short duration, and WhiteChips would have blown them out of the water when its new generation was ready. Even with the atypical delays in development and manufacturing, WhiteChips was still in basically good shape for the long haul.

However, WhiteChips needed both the right quality and quantity of people to make it work, as the history of prior introductions showed, although this was ignored by Jack. In the name of reengineering-induced cost-cutting, the company had neither when the moment of truth arrived. And throughout this painful time, WhiteChips' managers were tied up fighting fires inside the company just when they should have been fighting battles in the marketplace. WhiteChips needed change but it also had a natural absorption rate.

In the movie "The Great Escape" the Nazis funnel hundreds of escape-minded Allied prisoners into a specially secured, supposedly escape-proof concentration camp. Instead of discouraging escape, this move only serves to concentrate an enormous amount of talent in one place – enough to outmaneuver all the security precautions. As WhiteChips unleashed change trigger after change trigger, its competitors grew used to dealing with the constant disruptions. Although they did not have WhiteChips' technological lead, they did have enough talent and firing-line experience to survive and take advantage of WhiteChips' mistakes. Thus, while WhiteChips was construed as the change-ready organization incarnate, actually its competitors should have been accorded that distinction. They had grown nimble and agile, wily and shrewd by necessity. Like the boxer fighting a slugger, they learned how to respond with their wits – through pricing, product innovations, sales and marketing, and, above all, superb market intelligence.

As a result, competitors knew as soon as WhiteChips began to falter, and were able to zoom new chips into the market, despite the realistic assumption that their edge would be short-lived. The case of WhiteChips serves as a cautionary tale of what can happen when a company takes its eyes off the market and buys into yet another fad.

# 4 Taking Control of the Organization

WhiteChips lost its way not because it didn't take control, but because it never had control in the first place. The organization blinded itself to that reality because it offered – both to itself and to the outside world – the image of being a jewel of great control. That self-created image also made WhiteChips most vulnerable to a precipitous fall when it hit on an apparently insolvable problem – but the irony is that the problem could have been easily overcome if the right control mechanism had been in place.

WhiteChips fooled itself, and everybody else, because Jack White seemed to be in control – with his majority stock ownership, technical genius, and leadership driving the endless number of chip generations that destroyed the competition before it even reached the playing field. Yet any semblance of control was illusory. Jack worked hard in the labs and left all other functions of the organization to other people. Most of the supporting cast was rarely on the same page. Hank and Mark came closest to working together, but largely on an ad hoc, not on a systematic, basis. Bob was in a world of his own, pinching pennies when he should have been overseeing a prudent investment policy crafted in conjunction with Hank, Mark, and the other managers based on their real needs. Sadly, nobody ever set him straight, although admittedly Jack was the only one who could have done that. Barbara, despite some laudable qualities, had abrogated any opportunity to become a genuine contributor to the business success of WhiteChips by keeping a low profile when she could have been a full member of the team, and perhaps a catalyst for greater cohesion of the disparate parts.

As a result, WhiteChips was a highly fragmented organization. No one cared about the problem, as long as they were able to remain on top. Why argue with success? The ultra-loose, unconnected mode of independent fiefdoms worked fine when everything was going well, but broke down completely at the sign of the first crisis.

WhiteChips learned the hard way about the harsh penalties for corporate fragmentation because it lacked a coordinated problem solving capability; when a problem did emerge, it was magnified and panic reigned. This made WhiteChips vulnerable to the blandishments of the RAICers – Mr. Inside, Bob, and Mr. Outside, Jim. Ultimately, WhiteChips ceded control of the entire organization to those least qualified to hammer out a real solution to the margin problem. WhiteChips is representative of many companies that are experiencing the crisis of control.

While supporters of deengineering bristle at the thought of imposing hard and fast tenets, there are a few rules that managers can consider to ensure that they are in control of their organizations:

### Beware of RAICers Bearing Fads

The first rule is to recognize the RAICer, and to spot the RAICer for what he is selling. Beware especially of the RAICer who is ready with an off-the-shelf solution before he even looks into the problem – or comes back with the cure after a cursory examination. That's a tip-off to expect trouble. If you, as an expert, know a problem is deep and complex, how can an outsider produce such a quick fix? And if you can identify the RAICer, chances are you will be able to come up with the solution on your own – a solution that will probably be simple, straightforward, unvarnished, and easy to execute.

### Stress Simplicity and Clarity

Be aware of what you face by heeding the RAICer with a set of universal panaceas in his kit bag. The RAICer is liable to confuse the issue, and substitute complexity for simplicity. The RAICer is likely to slow down the process, at a time when speed and a direct approach is needed. If the process is complex, the RAICer will have to be present for a long time to make sure it's done "his way." And if execution is slow, the RAICer has to stay with it even longer, thus extending his billable hours. All of that imbeds excessive and unneeded costs into the process – from the missed opportunity costs because the process was too slow, to the huge tab run up by the RAICer.

## Be Sensitive to Conflicts of Interest

Beware, as well, of the RAICer who is not only self-perpetuating but who also perpetuates the process on behalf of others. Be suspicious of the academic who delivers a managerial concept but needs to hand the action phase off to consultants, industrial engineers, information systems specialists, or human resources mavens. Nevertheless, the clock keeps ticking, and their cash registers keep ringing. And watch for the sponsor – the member of your management team who is sponsoring the RAICer. He may be an in-house RAICer – like Bob – summoning an outside RAICer. He may, in fact, be anathema to your efforts to take control.

## Look for Real Problems and Experts

Conversely, learn to recognize and properly use inside advisors and outside consultants who are not RAICers. They will come with no preconceived notions, and will be willing to work with you on a customized solution. Your knowledge of your company and your market – translated into real managerial control – should be able to tip you as to whether the outsider is working for you or not.

The non-RAICer will keep it simple, so you can get right to work on your problem, and be ready to handle the next one that will inevitably emerge. Keeping it simple is an intriguing tenet for operating the company internally as well. It is the essence of concentrating an attack on a complex problem. Ironically, however, complexity may be the product of people, who, through inefficiency or design, make things complex.

Take the case of the automobile company that was having problems with the seams on its visors. The engineers decided to reengineer the manufacturing process and develop a new seam. They hired a consultant and created a team to diagnose the cause of the problem and redesign an end-to-end solution. No one thought about why the defect had not appeared before (a classic RAICer approach). The company's president suggested that they investigate the issues before proceeding. In a few days, they found that a faulty machine in the factory of a subcontractor was creating the defect. For a nominal fee the company worked with the subcontractor and the machine was repaired. The president's simple request avoided a RAICer attack.

## Manage the Consultants

Once consultants have been enlisted, work closely with them. Get progress reports and, perhaps most important, if a number of different consultants are working on different areas at the same time, coordinate all their efforts to make sure they are working together and contributing to a unified attack on your problem.

Know when things are being dragged out too long. Don't be afraid to call a halt, even if the consultant tells you the investigation is not completed and he does not have enough information. An incomplete process that speeds a response may be better than prolonged delays.

## Practice Due Vigilance

Exercise great care in selecting your consultants. Practice "due vigilance." Check out the advisor's references with prior clients. Have these consultants actually done this specific type of work before? Have they delivered usable recommendations that achieved tangible results? Are they credible? Are they objective? Are they in tune with a change-responsive organization? Are they working for you or for themselves? Do they have a tendency to bring in an army of specialists who will run up the bill? Would their previous clients use them again? Do they tend to offer off-the-shelf solutions or specifically tailored approaches that a business really needs to counterattack the effects of a change trigger? Do they understand the concept of responding quickly and restabilizing the organization, so it can continue to stress growth and sharpen its competitive edge? Have individual consultants published books or articles on the subject?

## Eliminate the Residue of Failed or Incomplete Change Initiatives

Organizations typically spend a great deal of time selling a change initiative but little time auditing its effectiveness. Successful organizations must initiate, and institutionalize objective assessments of their initiatives. These assessments must be based on the organization's strategic framework. The organization should utilize its most change-oriented employees, at all levels, to screen all existing initiatives, with the expressed goal of eliminating those that are inconsistent with the requirements of its strategic framework. This will unclog the organization's arteries, and free it to meet future challenges. There should be no sacred cows! This process of elimination should not be limited to change initiatives – it should also include both internal and external members of the RAICer complex.

Dennis Buchert, chief banking officer of IBJ Schroeder, says, "Stay away from fads and take the hard way out by analyzing your situation, and possibly reinventing a new wheel if necessary. Fads automatically stifle mental thought processes; they are the quick fix." Also remember, as one CEO told us, "If I have to wait for the clipboard-carrying, MBA kids from a consulting firm to tell me what to do with my company, I might as well pack it in."

## Establish Clear Accountability for Results
## Throughout the Organization

John Georges, former chairman of International Paper, says, "The best place to assign accountability is through the performance management system. This key process should be tied to the company plan. Every individual must have a set of measurable goals that cascade down from the company's strategies. Everyone should be accountable for, and evaluated against, these measures, regardless of whether they serve in an individual, collaborative, or team environment. Reward systems must be linked to achievement in areas of accountability at all levels."

There is nothing new about this approach, but companies need to learn to handle the process better, since it is a key determinant of sound business decisions. Before spending money and valuable time on exotic training programs, organizations should ensure that everyone can handle the performance management process. The performance management process includes strategic goals and measures which cascade down throughout the organization, performance appraisal, pay strategy, salary administration, and incentive plan administration. Leonard Abramson, founder of US

Healthcare Incorporated, says that assigning accountability through "fail-safe business measurement systems alerts executives to key problems, and forces them to accept accountability for their resolution."

The suggestions made here about taking back control of your organization represent only the first phase of a more comprehensive process to initiate and sustain the organization's growth. The remaining three phases are discussed in the balance of this book. They are:

1. Mastering the change process.
2. Building a change-responsive organization.
3. Building change-responsive people.

Collectively, these three phases represent a map for leading growth from within the organization.

# 5 Mastering the Change Management Process

WhiteChips was like a truck loaded with dynamite; one small bump can touch off a highly destructive explosion, and the resulting destruction is far out of proportion to the insignificant event that caused it. The difference is that the dynamite truck driver is aware of the consequences, and so tries to avoid even the smallest bump. WhiteChips not only had no idea of the disastrous consequences of a slip, it couldn't even tell the difference between a big and small bump – or whether there was any bump at all. It never recognized that modern companies are like dynamite trucks.

Despite its unbroken record of success, WhiteChips was organizationally flawed and virtually unaware of its defects, at least at the top, where knowledge of the problems was needed the most. It was ready to break at the slightest breeze, which in this case was whipped into a gale by a smooth-talking member of the RAIC complex.

WhiteChips was misaligned. Jack and the other top managers were so hung up on the technical side that they did not take proper account of manufacturing, sales, and other key organizational components. And when these sectors were vitally needed, they had been so decimated by reengineering that they were paralyzed.

WhiteChips took its eye off its market. It deluded itself into believing that it was in the "chips market." Given its record of being first and setting standards, that was not altogether wrong. But reality management based on deengineering would have indicated that at some stage, its utopian situation would alter, if not change completely. Change is a fact of competitive life.

WhiteChips had the wrong CEO. Jack White was an excellent engineer and a first-rate entrepreneur who kept the company centered on making waves and being first in a market where being top gun is crucial. But when the going got rough, his management style sapped the non-technical areas of the organization of needed vitality and talent, and he never fully appreciated their roles in making the good times so lush. He was willing to throw them to the dogs in the name of high technology and wide margins. He probably should have let someone else manage the company while he ran the technical side. This is not an uncommon situation in start-up technology companies (and even in larger, more mature companies), especially when constant change is forcing more and more CEOs to become change specialists.

In short, WhiteChips was not a change-oriented organization because it lacked a change management process, which would enable it to transform itself into a new entity. It also failed to recognize that growth requires continual adjustment of the company's alignment of strategy, operation, culture, and reward to stay in tune with a viable change management process.

### The Change Management Process

Like the muscle-bound giant at the other end of the business spectrum, WhiteChips had already passed through the first step of a four-phase change process but was shockingly unaware of the degree to which it had been destabilized. The four-phase process is depicted below and its relationship to the WhiteChips' situation is described on the following page.

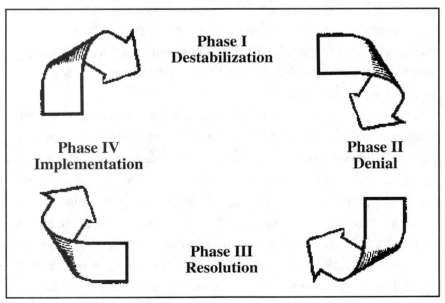

**Phase I**
**Destabilization**

**Phase IV**
**Implementation**

**Phase II**
**Denial**

**Phase III**
**Resolution**

## Phase I: Destabilization

WhiteChips' troubles began when it did not detect the threats and opportunities inherent in its business environment. These threats and opportunities are called "change triggers," and they can severely endanger – or enhance – an organization's potential for growth. Change triggers are the entry point into the process; they initiate the destabilization phase.

Typically, a change trigger is an external force, such as a competitor's introduction of a new product or technology, a change in the customer base, a shift in customer demand, or the entry of a new competitor. Major change also can be triggered when a company's strategy, operations, culture, or reward systems become out of sync with its business situation. While a change trigger creates a threat because it destabilizes the market for the company, it can also offer an opportunity. An intelligent reaction to the trigger will enable the company to take advantage of new developments for its economic and technological benefit.

The faster a company recognizes the trigger and moves to restabilize itself, the more competitive it will be, and the better prepared it will be for the next change trigger – internal or external. Ideally, an organization will be introducing change triggers rather than reacting to them.

WhiteChips was originally a change initiator. It was constantly creating change triggers and unleashing them on its competitors. Ultimately, the competitors learned to optimize their response to WhiteChips' tactical actions. While they could not match WhiteChips' proficiency at technical innovation, they became expert at translating WhiteChips' innovation into their own products, to meet customer requirements better, at attractive cost.

Why was WhiteChips unable to fully capture the value of its innovation? Jack White and his technical coterie were so enamored with their press clippings that they failed to recognize the substantive changes needed within the company to handle the external market change triggers they had created. Had they recognized this misalignment, they would have realized that an inevitable problem was looming, because of their neglect of manufacturing, sales, and the other components that are key to efficiently making, selling, and distributing the fruits of R&D's labors. A sound knowledge of this "value chain" would have enabled WhiteChips to specifically address its margin problems. Additionally, the company would have handled everything itself more quickly and simply – and avoided falling prey to an ill-fated, greatly flawed quick fix.

## Phase II: Denial

The most substantive problem faced by WhiteChips was its inability to take purposeful and concerted action as the forces of change swirled around it. It did not notice organizational destabilization until it was too late. WhiteChips had entered Phase II: Denial.

In simplest terms, Phase II is the zone of self-deception. A company that is too inept to cope with change or is highly change-resistant, either lacks the ability to discern a change trigger, or refuses to recognize the significance of the triggers it does detect. Such companies fail to realize that major change is inevitable. The longer a company remains in denial, the more at risk it is. Companies that quickly truncate this denial phase are likely to successfully restabilize themselves after a change trigger strikes, and reestablish their competitive advantage.

As WhiteChips pursued its program of "fad-based" change initiatives, it avoided the unmentionable question – what would happen if these initiatives did not work? WhiteChips had no early system to detect problems because it didn't think it needed such a "superfluous" resource. If such an intelligence operation had been in place, WhiteChips would have moved rapidly into Phase III: Resolution.

## Phase III: Resolution

Once a company perceives a change trigger, it must deal with it immediately. It must analyze its alignment to its market and make key change decisions to strategically position itself. Four change decisions are possible:

1. Linear change is a major move by the company within its primary market. This may be done in the change management context, for example, when a change trigger destabilizes a position in one market

niche. Rather than fight back directly, the company may find an opportunity in another niche. Most often, it tries to do a better job with its existing products in its existing markets.

2. Geometric change is what an individual company must execute to survive widespread changes in its industry or market, e.g., maturation of the U.S. computer and paper industries. This is a classic change management situation. Triggers affect just about everybody in the field. The affected firm can go linear or it can go to other game plans, such as expanding overseas with strong existing products. Most frequently, the firm tries to get bigger by acquiring market share in current and new markets.

3. Quantum change is when the company moves into a new, but related, market with a new, broader product line to support its existing business, e.g., a telecommunications company entering the computer field. The movement afield may be the result of a change trigger, or the converging company may itself create a change trigger.

4. Metamorphosis occurs when the company completely remakes itself in response to change triggers. Its old industry has become so hostile that it is no longer habitable, so an exit to another market is a good move. Remaking a company has change management elements at every turn; it involves new markets and new products, and probably will require new skills, e.g., conversion of the Greyhound Corporation, a transportation company, into Dial, a consumer products company.

These change decisions can only be made when the company is fully aware of what is happening in its markets and with its competitors.

*The Alignment Blueprint*
After making a strategic change decision, the organization needs to

specify and quantify the results it expects from the newly devised initiative. It must project a targeted growth rate and create a set of aligned strategic assumptions called a blueprint, an operating plan. The blueprint will sketch how the firm will achieve its growth rate, as well as the best means for preparing the organization to implement the plan. A blueprint embraces the following nine elements:

1. Mission/Vision: A synopsis of the markets or clients to be served, the business purpose of the company, the services or benefits the company will deliver to the market, the value to be provided to investors and employees, and the positioning of the company on the basis of where it wishes to be in its market.

2. Financial Goals/Measures: Appropriate financial goals and measures based on the expectations of investors or owners and the realities of the market (size, growth rate, competitive position, share). These goals and measures would include return on assets, return on investment, revenue growth, operating margins, etc.

3. Market Goals/Measures: Market positioning or progress based on corporate mission, financial resources, and market realities (competitive positioning). These market goals must include becoming number one in market share, market leadership, or operating margins or being the market's top generator of cash flow, etc.

4. Strategies: Specific long-term action plans designed to achieve financial and market goals based on clear success measures in accordance with the mission. Also included here are specific actions for utilizing human and physical resources, and community relations policies.

5. Core Competencies: The knowledge base designed to support the mission, achieve market goals, and execute business strategies.

6. Shared Values (Culture Measures): A common set of organizational expectations that drive, support, or guide the behavior of the company. These values typically include expectations for dealing with customers, employees, owners, and the community.

7. Market Distinctiveness: Unique aspects of the company within its marketplace (service, people, capital base, etc.).

8. Reward Strategies: Type and amount of compensation packages needed to reinforce business and human resources strategies.

9. Organizing Principles: The key organization structures and management processes needed to implement the strategies.

With the Alignment Blueprint in place, the final or action stage of the change management process – implementation – can be set in motion.

## Phase IV: Implementation

A truly change-responsive organization will compress the time between spotting a change trigger and implementing a full-scale response. Competitive advantage goes to the company that moves more quickly and effectively than its competitors who are jarred by the same trigger. The Alignment Blueprint is the foundation for the implementation phase. It is a working document – developed, understood, and recognized by all stakeholders. Typically, implementation plans include the following components:

1. Communication of the company blueprint to all stakeholders and solicitation of feedback on potential areas of implementation.

2. Introduction of a new performance management system to incorporate the strategic goals and measures aligned in the blueprint into the performance plan of every employee, and training of all employees in performance planning and appraisal.

3. Implementation of a new reward program to reinforce the new goals and measures, and training of all employees in how the reward system will be administered.

4. Embedding the core competencies and values described in the blueprint into selection, promotion, and retention processes; training all supervisors in new employee assessment methodology.

5. Utilization of new assessment methodology to position the most change-oriented people in key positions.

6. Realignment of management structures, practices, and processes around blueprint assumptions.

7. Codifying the change process to ensure continual monitoring of the environment to detect market, competitor, and internally driven change triggers.

8. Engaging in continual assessment of company positioning with respect to the goals and measures stated in the blueprint.

### The Tragedy of WhiteChips

WhiteChips' biggest blunder was not understanding the reality that it could lose a round. It stayed mired in its dream world – the zone of self-deception – because it did not understand its own targeted alignment. It lacked any semblance of a blueprint to tie its key components together. The company was wholly centered on the technical side. As long as it kept pumping out new developments, it would stay in front. This was nearest and dearest to the heart of the CEO, who saw the other parts of the organization as merely necessary means to an end. He liked the other people and didn't interfere with how they operated, but they knew that they never really counted in the same way that his cronies in the labs did. They were well paid, but mostly to keep quiet rather than to produce. While the lack of interference was generally welcome, it was construed more as benign neglect than a true vote of confidence. At the moment of truth these attitudes turned out to be correct, when Mark Rosenthal and Hank Messina fought a losing battle against Jim Clay's shrewd assessment of Jack White's prejudices.

If Mark and Hank are to be faulted, it is because they did not speak up earlier and let Jack and others know of their problems. But they were constantly under the gun to keep their own troops on the go, and, judging by the way they lost the reengineering battle, there is doubt that Jack would have listened to them sooner. Certainly, the cultural atmosphere wasn't conducive to their being given a real place at the hierarchical table.

Barbara doesn't escape criticism that easily. Yes, she wasn't enthusiastic about installing the linguistic and symbolic trappings of reengineering. And, yes, she refrained from trying to impose too much heavy-handed human resources orthodoxy on a creative organization. But she ceded too much authority and policy making to the operating people, letting them have their own way without any input from her group. She erred on the side of keeping such a low profile that she was almost invisible. The human resources chief should have been creating the cultural and policy framework to help the managers make sense of her decisions. Barbara was doing none of this. She was going with the flow, rather than helping regulate it. She had become virtually superfluous within WhiteChips and enjoyed no credibility when it was important for her position to be taken seriously.

In Jack White's view, WhiteChips told the market what to do. What the market really wanted was irrelevant, although in reality that was for Mark Rosenthal's salespeople to deal with on their own. The WhiteChips' case was a near-perfect argument for splitting the CEO's job from the chairmanship.

A president/CEO with the right peripheral vision could have not only kept the company in alignment and its eyes on the marketplace but also could have ensured that the alignment to market was in proper balance. Jack's hang-ups on the technical side blocked such a broad view. There's no guarantee that Jack would have been much of a chairman as change leader but at least he might have had more time to work on that role. Perhaps in the end, he might have had to replace himself as chairman to concentrate on his true love – the lab.

Ironically, WhiteChips was uniquely well-positioned below the executive suite to handle change. Line people like Mark Rosenthal and Hank Messina were so accustomed to having change triggers released from within that they were ready and willing to make the changes needed to keep WhiteChips in sync with the market. The problem was that, given Jack White's narrow view of success and Bob Rogers' penny-pinching sycophantism, their change initiatives never became visible to other people in the organization. Again, it was a primary example of a company badly misaligned, living on borrowed time.

Whether operating executives like Mark and Hank, or people specially designated to fulfill these roles, change leaders should be distributed throughout all levels of the company, and in the right mix. They are the movers, the drivers, the pushers of the change initiative growing out of the board and the market intelligence unit, and they get the message of change out to the troops. They are highly visible and in direct contact with the organization's people, and they lead by action rather than words. They monitor who is to be rewarded for change and they measure the success of the change initiative at the working level. It matters less exactly where they are placed or how they are titled than that they are in place and on hand. The change leaders are the apostles of deengineering.

# 6 Building the Change-Responsive Organization

Once an organization has built an Alignment Blueprint for growth, its success will be based on how well it synchronizes the four change elements – the strategic shell, flexible delivery system, change-ready culture, and contingent reward systems.

## The Strategic Shell

The change-responsive organization can create resilience – the ability to respond to change triggers quickly and effectively – through a framework of options and exit strategies called a strategic shell. The use of the right strategic shell enables the company to speed through the zone of denial and into the zone of implementation without skipping a beat. The existence of an exit strategy reduces much of the anxiety and uncertainty of change programs.

A well-built strategic shell requires a company to:

1. Create and communicate a blueprint of its nine key business assumptions. To ensure that the blueprint is always timely, it must be continually reviewed in the light of opportunities and threats. The nine key assumptions cover the areas of: mission/vision, financial goals, market goals, strategies to achieve the goals, core competencies, shared values, market distinctiveness, reward strategies, and organizing principles. All these assumptions must work together, and all goals must be ultimately tied to measures and standards of performance, based on a projected business situation.

2. Know and monitor all change triggers in the business environment, whether generated by customers, competitors,

51

suppliers, the target market(s), or the company's own efforts. In addition to basically beneficial developments generated from within the company, some internal change triggers can arise from inefficient operations, inappropriate culture, or unproductive reward systems that don't allow the firm to meet market needs.

3. Simulate a variety of destabilization possibilities from a wide array of actual and perceived change triggers (best case, worst case, etc.). Borrowing from the "games approach" and modern sensitivity analysis, this technique not only allows advance planning of appropriate actions but permits the visionary company to actually anticipate change triggers before they are unleashed, so the company can act ahead of them – a critical leg-up on competitors.

4. Ensure that any change initiatives reinforce complete internal alignment – of strategy, operations, culture, and reward – and that this "Total Company Alignment" confronts the new realities of the trigger-jolted market.

5. Support a top-notch information-gathering capability to track internal and external triggers, while supplying the board and change agents with correct data to make decisions for a quick resolution.

6. Use a change management process that (in the words of Harvard's Michael Beer) demands that managers "discuss the undiscussable." This is critical because the alternative to grappling with the unthinkable is the potentially disastrous assumption that "It can't happen to us." Thus, it can be the difference between getting through the four-stage change process quickly and rapidly restabilizing the company or losing precious time in the zone of denial. Such a process requires the company not only to tolerate, but to encourage, a full complement of change agents who thrive

on intelligent change initiatives. It also may require the company to internally create its own change-demanding crises to fight complacency (a technique advocated by Gary Fernandes of Electronic Data Systems).

7. Develop an exit strategy for every business, product, and person in the organization. This is the ultimate in planning, an indispensable cushion against potential destabilization – as well as an agent for causing destabilization for competitors. Exit strategies, designed well in advance, provide options when the change triggers hit, especially when the options or choices also create opportunities. The change response may fall short of actual exit but it is nice to have the most extreme of options available and planned out; it minimizes the pain and shock to the organization.

8. Establish and maintain a growth strategy of at least 5% more than your market; anything less will kill your company. As a play on the exit strategy and Fernandes' "crisis creation" approach, management may merge a fading company while it still has value, rather than reengineer it toward certain death.

9. Maintain a system for shifting resources quickly when a change trigger develops.

In examining the snapshot of an organization's strategic shell, the customer must answer eight questions about itself:

1. How effective is customer relationship management?

2. How sharp is market segmentation and focus?

3. Do the products and services have clear superiority that can be measured in terms of customer benefits?

4. Is there maximum use of scale (economy) of operation relative to the best competitor?

5. Is the work force superior in skills and capabilities compared with competitors' employees?

6. Is there truly competitive market management focusing on factors such as flexibility, constant market surveillance, and the use of clear benchmarks to test progress?

7. How strong is market positioning, based on product differentiation, low production and delivery costs, and other favorable characteristics?

8. Does management have a viable exit strategy for every product, unit, and function in the company?

### Flexible Delivery System

The flexible delivery system of a change-responsive organization involves the constant reassessment and redeployment, when necessary, of all elements in the value chain. Organizations continually seek faster delivery of products or services to the market – from supplier through customers – with the fewest resources. As part of our four-phase change model, the chain should be broken down and reassembled on a regular basis, even without an overt change trigger. The key is to do the job on a regular basis as a primary aspect of reassessing the Total Company Alignment in advance of destabilization – i.e., preventive medicine.

The change-responsive organization relentlessly measures and anticipates customer and competitor responses to various change alignment scenarios. This means putting a premium on developing an effective market intelligence system.

Furthermore, the organization monitors the logistics used for delivery of products and services to customers, to consistently guarantee peak performance throughout the chain. The organization focuses both on internal functions and on external aspects (vendors, third-party distributors) of the chain. In this regard, benchmarking can be critical to measure performance of competitors' current (and, if possible, future) value chains. Many companies fail to design a flexible value chain and delivery system for the long run, and therefore don't have the know-how to revise their delivery systems as needed, or even to determine whether their chain is in disrepair.

An organization must create organizational structures that promote alignment among the interdependent components of the value chain. This means smooth management of the linkages, or hand-off points, in the value chain (purchasing, manufacturing, logistics, marketing, selling). Later, we will discuss the need to measure and reward the units that meet at the hand-off points, based on their ability to deliver smooth interaction and seamless linkages.

The organization must introduce top-notch information systems, to generate the critical data needed for decision making that can be easily used by people at all levels. A change-responsive organization must be cast with the right performers from top to bottom, and the information systems are the unifying devices that are necessary to keep everyone reading from the same page. The right information system ties employees and managers not only to their operating systems but also to external forces, such as customer data and competitors' activities. We all know that an under-informed or ill-informed organization is prone to disastrous mistakes – it tends to be stuck in the zone of denial. Information systems are also an excellent way to measure market change triggers, to police and monitor the value chain, and to determine whether satisfactory progress is being made toward the goals established in the blueprint. They are superb tools for creating internal crisis, because organizations change most quickly when prodded by market-driven data.

Since information systems generally tend to be expanded to the point of incoherence, we usually review their operating components based on five principles of an integrated support system.

1. Who is the worker who will use the system?

2. What advice and knowledge does the worker require to do the work?

3. What is the work, and how do you measure its success?

4. What skills must the worker have to do the work?

5. What tools and methods will the worker use?

The organization must eliminate businesses and functions that don't meet its blueprint requirements. Extraneous operations can impede the organization when quick responses to change triggers are essential. Information systems should be based only on the firm's strategies, which everyone in a change-responsive organization should understand. They should not be loaded with extras that cast the information system or any other technology as an end in itself.

De-emphasis of staff functions, such as human resources, strategic planning, and finance, is mandatory. Emphasis should be on building the functional competency of the people who actually work in the value chain – especially those closest to the market. The managers of these functions should be allowed independence, particularly in making the critical decisions nearest to the customer. Small staff functions can be used for strategy and policy development, to create synergies between units, and to train and monitor line units. But all major human resources and strategic planning initiatives should be managed by line people, supported by functional specialists and simple communications programs.

An organization's value chain alignment can be analyzed by the following principles:

1. Anything that adds cost but not value to the firm's products is waste. The nature of competition will not tolerate waste; neither must we.

2. Low cost is a dependent variable; it results from doing things

well. Our goal is to always be the low-cost manufacturer or service provider in our marketplace.

3. Excess complexity in our products, procedures, or organization exponentially adds cost – both in dollars and time. Pursue simplicity as a key to competitive effectiveness.

## Change-Ready Cultures

No organization can use change management processes to effect proper alignment unless it has the support of most of its employees. Our research and experience has helped to broadly define five types of employees.

*Change agents* and *change managers*, the most admirable group, are the organizational leaders who envision, articulate, and communicate a vision and garner support from others. Another group, *change facilitators*, typically support the changes initiated by *change agents* and *change managers*, while *change buffers* and *change resistors* fight change.

*Change agents* are highly risk-oriented individuals who are skillful at detecting change triggers and predicting their impact on their organization. They work diligently to force the organization to respond, frequently jeopardizing their position. To be victorious in driving a response, change agents must have powerful sponsors who actively support and protect them. Well-managed companies value and legitimatize the role of change agents, particularly in strategic planning, product planning, research and development, and manufacturing. They require organization recognition and encouragement, because change agents can otherwise become company pariahs, because they deliver unpopular messages and can easily fall prey to a "kill the messenger" backlash.

*Change managers* are also risk-oriented individuals, but they will not go to the same extreme as change agents to advance their agendas. The strength of change managers lies in their ability to blend power conferred from above with respect from both peers and subordinates. While change agents rarely implement a change plan, change managers have the ability to formulate, structure, and implement a creative initiative quickly and decisively. While change agents will usually circumvent institutional structures to achieve results, change managers are adept at bending them to their advantage. Change managers frequently use change agents to drive a change, rather than assume the highest degree of risk themselves.

*Change facilitators* are the loyal troops of the change leaders. They take their cues from change agents and managers, and commit to the programs once a clear statement of organization benefit is made. Change facilitators help create a change-responsive organization, because they truly support a change effort, rather than blindly obey.

*Change buffers* are passive change resistors. They don't like diversion from the status quo and will get in step with a change initiative only under duress. They deny the need for change, and typically block the communication process. They are apt to require extensive studies with large task forces, and the extensive involvement of consultants, to justify even a small organizational remodeling. Yet, change buffers can sometimes serve a constructive role, by forcing the organization to consider all options before taking action. Only a small number of individuals with this style can be tolerated, since they can choke an organization's capacity to respond quickly.

*Change resistors* are the least tolerable member of the change-ready work force. They actively crusade against organizational transformation. They believe that any uprooting of the status quo will have a personal adverse impact. Change resistors are internal terrorists, and they can exacerbate the destabilizing impact of change triggers. They actively work to keep the company in denial. All change resistors and most change buffers should be purged from the organization.

Each stage of business growth requires a different mix of managerial styles. The faster the growth rate, the greater the number of change agents and managers required. For real change to occur, an organization must be almost entirely composed of change agents, managers, and facilitators. One of the great failures of reengineering is traced to an inability to significantly increase the number of change leaders and facilitators before organization transformation is attempted.

## Movement Within the Change-Ready Organization

The change-ready organization moves people frequently to new positions, by plan. Otherwise, people become too well-entrenched to recognize and cope with the demands of change. Like a tennis or baseball player who is always anticipating the next play, employees must define their careers in terms of the future, rather than the past. Companies can foster future-oriented thinking by not keeping any employee in a given job for long, but these frequent moves must be planned and communicated. Employees must understand that today there is no such thing as job security, only employment security, and that their best preparation for change is a strong resume that shows lots of diversity. The company must respond by managing its work force so that it retains as many high-potential or peak-performing employees as possible.

In the 1970s, CPC International practiced this "planned readiness" approach. Years ahead of its time, it employed a "worldwide management audit" twice a year to determine each manager's readiness status. This screening process evaluated each employee in relation to the current and future requirements of the organization. To create a systematic program to match needs with available talent, every manager's career was projected between one and three organization levels, and all positions had an identified succession plan. Once a year, all the findings were reviewed by the chairman, Jim McKee, through at least five levels down in every business unit. This management audit also addressed a wide variety of human resources issues, such as affirmative action, performance assessment, culture fit, training, education, and development. This simple tool was thus the wellspring of personal career planning and management development. The worldwide human resources staff consisted of two professionals and one administrator who were there to help – not to dictate to – the operational staff who implemented the audit.

Through the use of these management audits, it became clear that every CPC employee had to have a personal exit strategy (e.g., up, sideways, or out), and that the company had to train each employee in the skills and methodologies of career planning before it was necessary for an outplacement firm to do so. Actually, because of the intimate relationship between the firm and its managers, the company was continually acting as an outplacement service (but doing the job better). We have also used this approach extensively in other organizations, to ensure that the company and its people were in a continual state of change-readiness.

## Contingent Reward Systems

Reward systems are essential if the company wishes to respond to changes in the alignment of strategy, operations, and culture. These systems use pay to plug a key gap and allow all elements of the company to function in complete synchronization. Reward systems are the incentives and reinforcers of a pay-for-performance culture. More specifically, compensation must become a reinforcement for the performances that make change work.

Rewards must be aligned with change readiness on at least two levels. First, variable pay can be used to promote correct behavior and to reward its results. It becomes an incentive to ensure that correct behaviors are sustained. Second, the contingent pay system must be correct in that it must fully jibe with the company's strategy, operations, and culture.

Each business situation requires a unique contingent pay strategy, which can be adapted frequently. The following two pages illustrate the types of options relevant to different business situations, various plans, and the conditions under which they operate.

The focus is on the use of variable pay plans to identify, motivate, and reward the results that drive the attainment of business goals. Since business situations change frequently, an organization must not lock itself into a rigid long-term program, and its work force must be conditioned to accept new and revised programs when new conditions mandate them.

WhiteChips made no provision for adjusting its pay systems in response to its changing business situation. Worse yet, it had no idea that revamping its reward programs was necessary.

# Business Situations and Contingent Reward Systems

## Targeted Individual Incentives – General

**Business situation:** Performance focus; affordability; goals and measures focus.

**How these incentives work:** Develop a pool or fund based on affordability, performance, and pay and distribute this pool to employees once a year; threshold must be reached before a payout can be made; typical focus is on financial measures resulting from cascading goals; formula for payout ties to specific goals and measures; total value of pool ties to total compensation levels; funds allocated on the basis of individuals or groups.

**Conditions for success:** Risk-accepting or entrepreneurial culture; measurable results and good follow-up; attainable goals; individuals influence results.

**Risks:** Organization doesn't define performance measures; entitlement culture resists risk-based pay; decisions are not under employee control; organization unable to objectively judge performance.

## Targeted Individual Incentives – Piece Rate

**Business situation:** Need to motivate employees in de-skilled environment.

**How these incentives work:** Pay individuals for each unit produced based on predetermined amounts for each unit (typically sole performance measures); differentiate base rate on levels of production; create a clear link between pay and performance.

**Conditions for success:** Simple, repetitive manufacturing process; results of work are easy to measure; minimum amount of interdependence; minimum need for cooperation; trust; job security.

**Risks:** Employees create counterproductive behavior trying to "beat the system;" high costs to maintain the incentive system (every technological change or new product requires new rates).

## Targeted Individual Incentives – Measured Day

**Business situation:** Inappropriate condition for piece rate; long job cycles.

**How these incentives work:** Fixed pay, assuming employees maintain a specific level of performance; guaranteed incentive payment in advance; pay does not fluctuate in the short term.

**Conditions for success:** Total commitment of management and employees; effective work measurement and control system; logical pay structure.

**Risks:** Worker ingenuity has lowered the standard; relieves pressure to perform; escalates labor cost (additions to staff).

## Key Contributor

**Business situation:** Strong need for an innovation culture; retention is imperative for key employees; business is in growth stage; special pay market conditions exist.

**How these incentives work:** Individuals with historical high performance are priced in plan (usually in technical hierarchy); special compensation in stock and cash in addition to traditional pay is given; there is usually a waiting period to receive the award.

*...Business Situations and Pay for Contingent Reward Systems (continued)*

**Conditions for success:** Ability to clearly identify "must-keep" employees; environment must provide for individual contribution; employee has resources and can influence resources.

**Risks:** Selection of recipients not creditable; nonrecipients may be discouraged.

## Gain Sharing, Rucker, Scanlon, Improshare

**Business situation:** Need to improve productivity and quality; shrinking margins; focus on information-sharing, employee commitment, involvement, and teamwork; interdependency of work assignments.

**How these incentives work:** Rewards quality, production, project milestones, or other financial or operational objectives; "shares" profit according to pre-determined formula (Rucker - production costs; Scanlon – labor costs; Improshare – hours worked); targeted incentive awards (5% to 7%).

**Conditions for success:** Management credibility and trust; employee opportunity to impact and improve; sufficient demand and market potential; work force interdependence; adequate support systems; management acceptance of employee work; commitment to change; strong measures.

**Risks:** People can't work together; lack of top management commitment; use as a "band-aid"; inadequate design, administration, and follow-through; lack of understanding of risks; payouts for gains are not a result of employee efforts; weak measures.

## Cash Profit Sharing

**Business situation:** Underachieving financial performance; need for lower relative labor costs; desire to create sense of common fate; shift from entitlement mentality to performance; quality orientation.

**How these incentives work:** Share the profit once a year; profit can be taken as cash, deferred for retirement, or split between the two options; promotes employee involvement in improving profits.

**Conditions for success:** Sense of common fate; management credibility and trust; employee involvement; open communications; "accurate" financial statements.

**Risks:** Profitable years are rare; employees view plan as a benefit; link between individual payout and organization performance is weak; expectations are not met; management uses the plan as a low-pay supplement; application is forced; employees focus on short-term results; uncontrollable factors exist that adversely impact profits.

## Pay for Knowledge or Skill (Competencies)

**Business situation:** Large skilled, technical, or professional work force and/or presence of career ladders; focus on work teams and need for work force flexibility; slower growth rates and fewer opportunities.

**How these incentives work:** Determine pay progression based on competency to perform multiple jobs.

**Conditions for success:** Well-defined position competencies; value person, not job; well-developed training and assessment programs; willingness to pay for unused capacity.

**Risks:** Weaken the pay-for-performance link; majority of employees with limited growth opportunities; unaffordable labor cost; investment on faith.

## Competency-Based Pay

One of the myriad RAICer scams that have appeared in the last five years is the overselling of competency-based pay. Competency-based pay is founded on the quest for finding underlying attributes or qualities that have a demonstrated relationship to superior job performance (a specific organizational result). Competencies describe what people know and/or can apply based on observable behaviors. Once the competencies, or success factors, are expressed in behavioral terms, an administrative process is initiated to link the various competency levels to specific rewards. This compensation package assumes that supervisors are confident in the relationship between competencies and measurable results.

One of the worst results of not adjusting pay systems to other changes is that an organization may, at times, pay employees for competencies no longer required by their job accountabilities.

Competency-based pay contrasts with results-based pay, which measures what employees achieve based on a mutually agreed-upon set of goals and measures. "Why bother rewarding competencies when you can reward results?" is an intelligent question. But in the era of constant change, the use of competencies is most effective in the selection, training, and development of the employees needed to populate a change-responsive organization. The competencies spelled out in the company blueprint are accurate predictors of current and future organization success.

## Broadbanding

Another recent compensation fad is called "broadbanding." This is the process of collapsing a large number of salary grades into a few wide bands, presumably for the better administration of salaries in the condensed, flatter, leaner, meaner, and more market-oriented organization. While our estimate is that no more than 3% to 5% of all U.S. companies have experimented with this fad, RAICers have pursued it with fervor. Incredibly, at a time when companies should be devoting more of their effort to creating, making, selling, and distributing products in a competitive market, RAICers are diverting this energy into the task of collapsing their salary structures.

Since all pay structures are tied to external pay markets for specific jobs, it does not matter whether salary ranges are organized vertically, in small bands, or horizontally, in wide bands. Under deengineering, the company can have as many or as few grades as it likes – debating the number is a waste of time. At International Paper, former chairman and CEO John Georges designed the grade system in just two hours – and he did it a lot better than a compensation professional would have.

## Job Evaluation

Job evaluation is an important part of ensuring internal equity and market competitive pay, but spending a lot of time on job evaluation is usually counterproductive – a make-work activity for insecure compensation specialists and RAICers. It is a distraction for line managers, who should be able to evaluate and/or classify jobs within their organization by their relative contribution to the company or use benchmarking to relate jobs to similar positions in other companies. All they need is a simple but accurate job evaluation and survey system, training in establishing pay grades in accordance with the company's pay strategy, and general instruction in administering pay systems.

Due to the importance of pay systems in motivating employees, employee pay administration should be one of the criteria for evaluating every manager's and supervisor's performance. Thus, the function of job evaluation is moved from human resources to line management, where it makes more sense – on the line, closer to the market. Nevertheless, human resources should retain responsibility for system selection, guidance, and training. Any line manager who cannot handle salary administration is not doing a vital part of the job. Human resources has become an excuse for lack of trust in line managers to perform their performance management functions; lack of trust is the enemy of the change-responsive company.

# 7 | Building Change-Responsive People

A change-responsive organization is only as change-responsive as its people. To redirect and realign an organization to succeed in an era of rapid change, a modern company must be filled with, and led by, truly change-responsive people. The company's role models must be the employees who are taking the critical actions at the cutting edge of change.

To review, the key characteristics of a change-responsive organization are that it is imbued with a change-driven culture with a clear sense of direction, and a collaborative environment that encourages people to work together for beneficial change. To promote these critical cultural attributes, keep the field of change consistently fertile, and execute the change initiative, the organization needs a substantial proportion of change agents, the actual drivers of change: change managers, who drive the myriad implementations touched off by the agents, and change facilitators, who get themselves, their systems, and their operations smoothly in line with the change initiative. The change-responsive organization must also reduce the number of employees who are change-resistant: the change buffers, who passively resist change, and, worse yet, the change resistors, who actively work to defeat change.

There is no set number or proportion of change agents, managers, and facilitators that is applicable to every situation. Determining the best ratio for the company is one aspect of deengineering. The ratio is dependent on the organization's size, growth rate, stage in the business cycle, and the speed with which it must respond to a change trigger. In general, faster growth requires more flexibility, and a higher ratio of change-driven people. Yet, more important than their number is that the agents, managers, and facilitators of change be in visible, key positions. Their functions must be clearly understood and communicated. They must be recognized as leaders and they must be respected by their charges.

No change initiative can be executed effectively without a sufficient number of agents, managers, and facilitators. The change-responsive organization must actively maximize the number of change-oriented people by identifying and advancing change-minded employees, using change-responsiveness as a criterion for recruitment, retraining change-resistant behavior, and eliminating those who continue to resist change. These tactics require careful management of the gatekeeper processes of recruitment, succession, and termination.

The change agents, managers, and facilitators need not conform to any official company labels or titles; they can be identified by their action style and their recognition as change drivers by the organization. However, the most charismatic change enthusiasts must be in leadership positions. Conversely, change-resistant individuals must not inhabit the top ranks of the organization. Unfortunately, in many organizations, resistance is dug in at the highest tiers; these are the companies that experience the most difficulty adapting to change. Change-resistant CEOs and COOs may give lip service to the need for change, but they are prone to misguided responses and will promote, hire, and reward change resistors. No one else in the company will be fooled by the propaganda, and they, too, will resist change.

Although recently acclaimed as a great comeback story, not long ago IBM Corporation was a basket case. Its problems began with the repositioning of change-resistant top executives operating in the zone of denial. Despite continuing technological innovations, top management believed that IBM Corporation was impregnable, even in the midst of radical change. The company dogma was that its products were so good, its prices so competitive, its distribution and marketing so dominant, that it would sail blissfully through the rough seas of change. However, this perspective was the product of its own legend. As low-priced computers increasingly began to penetrate the market, IBM went into a free-fall.

IBM was so mired in the zone of denial that its change-resistant leaders refused to see that its position was collapsing, and its change-resistant board took too long to remove them. Only after new management, headed by a recruited change agent, was installed could the company muster its

66

considerable strength for a counterattack.

## Behaviors of Change-Responsive People

Our experience, combined with research on successful organizations, indicates that change-responsive people exhibit ten behavior traits. These ten traits are:

1. Optimism – positive and enthusiastic; will accomplish goals despite adversity.

2. Risk-Taking – takes risks, and defies established conventions.

3. Conscientiousness – keeps promises and commitments.

4. Responsibility – accepts responsibility to produce results.

5. Persistence – perseveres to accomplish objectives despite obstacles and challenges.

6. Vision – has a long-term view for self and the organization.

7. Focus – stays on course despite distractions and interruptions.

8. Leadership – influences and inspires others to follow their lead.

9. Candidness – provides honest feedback to others in the organization in a positive and supportive way.

10. Social Agility – exhibits social behavior that facilitates productive working relationships.

When an organization is composed of individuals who display these behaviors, it is change-responsive. Those who exhibit these behaviors most frequently are the change leaders (agents and managers). Those who demonstrate low levels of these behaviors are the change buffers and resistors.

No change initiative will succeed unless the organization is change-responsive. Evaluating a work force for these behaviors is essential before starting a change process in the organization.

## Change-Responsive Top Executives

For our newsletter, *The Change Manager*, we assessed more than fifty CEOs of large companies who had successfully implemented change initiatives. In each case, we found high change scores on each of the ten behaviors. We also found that the stronger the growth of the company, the stronger the CEO's change orientation. In fact, it is hard to think of a successful CEO today who has not demonstrated most of these behaviors. These essential attributes must permeate the change-responsive organization.

For example, John Georges, former chairman and CEO of International Paper, was dedicated to driving his company into a global position while maintaining a growth rate that exceeded the rest of the paper industry. Betsy Cohen of Jefferson Bank has a clear vision for transforming the banking industry, and the persistence to drive her vision. Frank Perdue's zest for quality drove Perdue Farms Incorporated's advances in the poultry business by converting a commodity into a brand.

Each of these leaders has not only demonstrated the willingness to take risks and accept the responsibility for achieving results but has coupled it with a clear vision that is unambiguously communicated throughout the organization. All of these successful people manage their different businesses with a commitment to change management.

## The Individual as a Self-Owned Business

To be truly change-responsive, people must think of themselves as self-employed. Cliff Hakim, in his excellent analysis of the individual's place in the modern organization, *We Are All Self-Employed*, posits the movement of the person from the "employed attitude," working for the company, to the "self-employed attitude," supplying skills and services to the organization as a contractor or, at least conceptually, as a quasi-outsourcer.

Hakim likens the "employed attitude" to a dependent mind-set and the "self-employed attitude" to an independent mind-set. The same subject is explored in Richard Bolles' *What Color Is Your Parachute?* He advances the idea of having an exit strategy that can be executed at the most propitious time.

Many people read these books too late – when they are unemployed or burned out. The right time to read them and take advantage of their guidance is when a person is successful, achieving peak performance, and progressing along a career path precisely on plan, because this is when one has the most leverage for self-marketing.

Before a person can be self-employed, he or she must be self-reliant. In an article in the April 1994 issue of *Fortune* Magazine, Walter Kiechel III stresses the need for self-reliance. He points out that self-reliance requires individuals to be adaptable – equipped to handle a multiplicity of roles on behalf of themselves as well as the organization. Thus, the truly self-reliant person is simultaneously an expert (in one discipline or more) and a generalist (capable of handling many disciplines), while exhibiting the traits of both a team leader and a team player as the occasion demands. A tall order? Certainly! Anyone who masters all these requirements must feel like the crew of the Starship Enterprise – going where no one has gone before.

Yet Kiechel offers a wake-up call to anyone who believes that he or she can ignore personal diversification in the modern marketplace. No one is going to give you a job forever, Kiechel warns. Anyone who believes otherwise is mired in a personal zone of denial, and needs to truncate it quickly by using his or her skills, talents, and traits to construct a personal exit strategy – which may involve moving to a new position in the company, changing careers or professions, or jumping to a new organization. As Dana Mead of Tenneco Corporation indicates, "There is no such thing as job security, only employment security." This can also be interpreted as creating a competitive resume in a growth market.

## Company Responsibility for Developing Self-Reliance

Aside from using his or her wits or instincts, how does the employee gain the skills and knowledge needed to engage in such a sophisticated exercise in self-directed career development? The answer is that the employee should not do it alone. The employee must receive considerable reinforcement from the company in developing self-reliance. Companies must start by cultivating the employee's skills of self-reliance with training and development. They must reinforce this concept with honest communication about the uncertainty of the modern employment situation, no matter how strong the performer or how much he or she has contributed to the organization. It is in the interest of the organization to train employees to develop a personal change model. Programs to help the worker surf the increasingly unstable labor market should be an integral part of a company's human resources program, and their expense should become a built-in cost of doing business. In turn, career development skills should be part of the core competency of every employee at every level of the organization.

If this sounds a bit radical – if it shakes up established paradigms of employee relations, and even seems like a road map for disloyalty, we can only say that an era of constant and rapid change has shattered those traditional beliefs. As times have changed, so has the impact of change triggers on working people. The time has come to be realistic about the job market and understand the mobility as we approach the 21st century (and even wanderlust) that is evolving. The employee who was once considered a gypsy for constantly shifting employers may be the model employee of the 21st century. If this is the case, then it is up to companies to take action, with promotions, salary increases, and recognition, to "body-check" the best of these gypsies.

Perhaps if auto workers and other vulnerable employees in the downsized smokestack industries had enjoyed personal mobility as a core competency and had experienced the career development process, they might have been better able to adjust to the upheaval in their industries. The cost-cutting reductions in work forces, the shift of manufacturing processes to other countries, the growth of outsourcing, and the cyclical nature of their industries would all have been recognized as change triggers and dealt with accordingly.

While Lance Berger was director of human resources at Corn Products, then a division of CPC International, he was part of a team that restructured the work force in response to competitive pressures, new technology, and a shrinking market. Sadly, it was his job to notify hundreds of employees that they were being laid off. He vividly recalled Charlie, a fifty-eight year-old market research manager, who had worked for the company for seventeen years telling me that he never thought he would ever be dismissed. The irony was that he had supplied the information that had helped form the downsizing decision that had led to his separation.

Charlie had no exit strategy, and never thought he would ever need one. He had been operating in his own zone of denial. Had he developed and practiced an exit strategy, he would have been able to truncate his denial zone and position himself for other job markets. However, this story does have a happy ending; Charlie went back to being a sugar trader, and eventually retired from that position at age seventy-five. Lance had convinced him to develop an exit strategy for his new career, which included a retirement plan.

## The Personal Change Model

Once the change-responsive person has put a fine edge on his or her career plans, by embracing the notion of de facto self-employment, he or she is free to consider all the options available under a well-conceived exit strategy. An adaptation of the change-response cycle that governs the actions of companies, the Berger Corporate Change Model encourages the individual to:

1. Assess and adjust his or her behavior according to the ten personal change dimensions, to advance personal change-readiness to the highest possible level. Change buffers and resistors will have the most difficulty changing their behavior and adopting an exit strategy.

2. Continually check the strength of the current job market, both internally, within the company, and externally, at other potential sources of employment. This ongoing assessment will determine

both the number and the growth prospects of potential opportunities that fit the individual's current and future values and competencies. A suggested rating scale is: three or more opportunities, a strong market; two opportunities, a moderately strong market; one or none, a weak market.

3. Determine the strength of the competition in these markets by measurements such as the quality of the other people compared with your skills and talents, and the number of opportunities – oversupply (more qualified people than positions), supply/demand balance, or undersupply (fewer people than positions). The strongest situation for the individual is undersupply – a seller's market – which also means that the potential competitors are less qualified, less skilled, or less experienced. In the weakest market – a buyer's market – a lot of people with equal skill levels are shooting for a few opportunities. In the worst case, many competitors have higher skill levels and qualifications than the individual doing the assessment.

4. Classify the individual's career by its progress and current status Is it in a growth stage, or has it plateaued with no advancement in sight? Is it in decline, as manifested by being passed over for promotions, answering to less experienced new supervisors, or suffering because its business area is not being nourished by new investments, or because of stagnation or erosion of the business itself?

5. Prepare a plan to position the individual in the correct job market (internal or external) to make the most of existing competencies or allow development of new competencies that will deliver optimal rewards for achievement. This plan can become an exit strategy, if needed, and can become the cornerstone of a personal strategy to market the individual in line with the selected exit/advancement option.

For these efforts to be effective, they must be performed on a continual basis; the assessments must constantly be done, the options must regularly be evaluated and tested, the exit strategy and personal marketing plan must continually be refined.

## Questions for Framing a Change-Responsive Plan

A series of questions can put a different spin on framing a change-responsive plan and personal exit strategy. These questions are applicable to anyone who works for a living, from the lowest rung of the organization to the top executive:

1. Do I have a mentor – someone I can talk to about my career in total confidence?

2. Do I have sponsors who will promote my career aggressively? (the more sponsors the better – multiple sponsors reduce risk).

3. Do I have a network of contacts within the company?

4. Do I have a network of contacts outside of the company?

5. Do I know the full range of opportunities within and outside of the company that I can compete for now and in the future?

6. Do I know the other people who can compete for the posts I want? Do they qualify, what are their capabilities, and how do they compare with me?

7. Am I expanding my credentials and my resume with increasingly important assignments each year? Can I differentiate myself from others, including my competitors?

8. Have I planned and developed my career over time?

9. Do I like my boss?

10. Am I comfortable in my current job?

11. Do I have an exit strategy?

12. Would I score high on the dimensions of change-readiness?

If you have answered "no" to any of these questions, and scored low on the change-readiness dimensions, you are prone to destabilization by internal or external change triggers that can arise from anywhere – from the marketplace to internal policy shifts. The more "no" answers you have, the greater your degree for personal destabilization and risk.

The positive news is that this exercise helps you make both a qualitative and quantitative assessment of your personal situation and provides the impetus for altering your situation. The choices are evident. Change the situation so that the "no" responses become "yes" responses, or develop an exit strategy posthaste and execute it.

# Part Two

# Change Managers in Action

The executives included in this section have appeared in
*The Change Manager* newsletter.
Each, faced with an internal or external change trigger that
buffeted his or her company, exhibited a willingness
to take risks and lead a major change initiative.

———————————

# William Benac
### Electronic Data Systems Corporation

When he took over the leadership of Electronic Data Systems' treasury group, William Benac was handed a double-barreled change management challenge. His most direct mission was to turn around a unit plagued by lackluster performance and low morale while, over the longer term, gearing the treasury group to offer more services to support the company's change in strategic direction and preparing the financial people for the coming spin-off of the firm by General Motors Corporation. The treasury group change process began under the umbrella of a corporate-wide leadership transformation effort, which strongly encouraged all executives to examine and enrich the effectiveness of their respective units.

After five years, Benac can point to such indicators of success as a 400% increase in productivity with one-third fewer workers, as well as a host of new services (commercial paper financing, bond and long-term debt management, pension plan management) in line with the company's doubling of its size.

Not that it was easy to achieve. Benac's measured and focused improvement program often ran into trouble. In the final analysis, success was achieved by keeping it simple – but keeping at it. The emphasis was to focus on achievable objectives and to communicate them and their progress to the work force. The primary areas of focus included:

> **Goal-Setting**: Benac set the basic goals for the finance function, correlated with EDS' goals, and had employees sign onto them individually.

> **Ethical Goals**: Business objectives and ethical objectives had to be met at the same time.

**Personal Development Goals**: Every employee was required to develop goals that in effect represented "what they were going to do to improve themselves."

**Leadership Goals**: Managers were encouraged to specify how they would lead the people under them in a joint effort to improve their own performance, their subordinates' performance, and the group's performance.

**Performance Reviews**: Ratings were accorded annually on the basis of reviews, and workers were encouraged to do self-evaluations.

**Career Development**: "People really needed opportunities to enrich their jobs and broaden their portfolios," says Benac, who believes in advancing people who are doing good jobs. Tuition reimbursements for professional education were offered and active membership in trade organizations was encouraged.

**Recognition**: People were provided with rewards for good performance – everything from notes of appreciation to monetary payments. Benac notes that he would rather pay people for performance as the year proceeds than pay out-sized bonuses at year-end.

While putting into practice a program distinguished by its alignment of the key elements of the organization, morale was helped by a strategy to avoid layoffs. The reduction in work force largely resulted from people transferring to other jobs in the company or leaving for other firms. In fact, when some people were fired for poor performance, their departures actually resulted in increased morale, suggesting that low performance and low popularity had coincided in these cases.

Before Benac hit pay dirt, however, he had some frustrating experiences that required him to change course. When he took over, an employee satisfaction survey confirmed that low morale was a problem, and harvested a host of suggestions for improving it. Benac acted quickly – setting up meetings to handle recommendations, getting plan timetables, sorting out action plans – but suffered a shock when another employee survey discovered continued unhappiness. The mistake, Benac says, was talking too much and not acting on the achievable.

"Things had improved, but we had talked so much about it that the level of expectation had also increased. People were no happier than they had been a year earlier." Yet, within three years, all the change indicators – performance, morale, and self-development – had improved dramatically, as the various change programs began to take hold.

*William Benac is currently with First Plus Financial.*

# Robert Bernstock
## Campbell Soup Company

Change management challenges can arise from an endless number of sources, including a company's own internally generated expansion plan. Campbell Soup Company found that out when it launched a program to expand its canned soup sales overseas and wound up creating an innovative way of generating premier rewards from the effort. Under the leadership of savvy overseas operations chief Robert Bernstock, Campbell instituted a daring new strategy of specially blending and customizing soups to the tastes of selected countries.

This refreshingly unique marketing plan demonstrates the worth of a major precept of deengineering – listen to the market. It also underscores how a deengineered program crafted by the organization itself can provide enormous room for creative thinking by the people who best know its markets. Best of all, Campbell's departure from the multinational norm of selling undifferentiated, mass-produced, commodity-type products everywhere in the world is working by almost every measure.

After inventorying its powerful assets and skills, Campbell decided to march to its own beat. The company, Bernstock notes, was able to leverage a leadership position in canned soups, a market in which its worldwide sales exceed all of its major competitors combined. It enjoys experience abroad, having established itself abroad many years before globalization was routinely attempted. It owns a network of plants around the world which could use more throughput to increase productivity. Campbell is also a skilled marketer that centers much of its efforts on wringing increased volume from the mature basic-soups business.

Campbell has a solid base for serving overseas markets in its own way and reaping the rewards from appreciative customers. Bernstock doggedly insisted that a customized program was what the markets were seeking. He concedes that many generic products, such as Coca-Cola and Kellogg Corn Flakes, can be sold almost anywhere without variation. "But when you are getting into main-course meals, you want to customize, because you are competing with thousands of years of history," he points out.

The Camden, New Jersey-based food company now offers an eclectic line of soups, including specially blended products for Mexico, pumpkin soup for Australia, onion soup for the United Kingdom, corn soup for Hong Kong, and pumpkin and corn soups for Japan. Overall, sales of the specially targeted soups have been growing at 10% to 15% annually, with earnings gains keeping pace. Two Campbell brands in Mexico are the third and fourth best-sellers, while the company's pumpkin soup is the market leader in Australia.

The flip side of the program, Bernstock candidly admits, is that it isn't easy to launch, manage, or expand. Bernstock describes customized markets as "time-consuming and painstaking." And in some areas, the going gets tougher, as Campbell has to keep on top of all sorts of cultural and religious nuances to win acceptance for its products. In Singapore, the smallest market penetrated with a targeted soup, Campbell had to set up special plants and institute special procedures to ensure the products are acceptable to Islamic consumers. "It is a painstaking process, but the good news is there are few companies in the world willing to be this customized and diligent in their efforts," he remarks.

One of his toughest selling jobs was to Campbell's own people. Initially, the proposal was greeted with "skepticism and disbelief" within the company. But success has been the ticket to buy-in, and Bernstock now has a large, enthusiastic army of rooters supporting expansion. "We have had so much success that we pretty much have advocates and champions of the system, including local overseas managers who see it as a way of growing revenue and building their business," he says.

Although the program is largely product-driven – the customized soup is created first – Bernstock insists that a Total Company Alignment be developed, albeit in a unique manner that befits the innovativeness of the entire marketing tactic. The program has actually spawned a series of mini

Total Company Alignments for each market it has penetrated, and this has helped increase support through multiple functions and levels. Initially, a market is selected, based on income, soup consumption, and other demographics. Next, Campbell determines the country's favorite flavor. Finally, such vital elements as research and development, manufacturing, marketing, and other functions are installed, piece by piece. "We build the infrastructure around our products," Bernstock notes.

As successful as the program has been, Bernstock says that it is only beginning and that expansion opportunities are vast. "We are only in about a dozen countries with this model now. We have one hundred eighty to go."

Campbell had a chance to go the standard homogenized route, but Bernstock exuded the confidence that Campbell had the ability to blaze its own international trail. His faith in Campbell's skills has proven him right.

*Based on an interview with LBA Consulting Group conducted in 1995, and an article appearing in the Summer 1995 edition of* The Change Manager.

# Robert Catell
## Brooklyn Union Company

Brooklyn Union Company, which recently entered its second century of operation, is about to take the most momentous step in its long history. In one of the myriad responses to the powerful change triggers buffeting the American utility industry, the venerable New York gas utility, which serves 1.1 million gas customers, expects to merge with neighboring Long Island Lighting Company in 1998 to form a giant company with diversified energy operations. The newly created company will have enormous physical assets, and a widespread core territory serving suburban Nassau and Suffolk counties on Long Island and the New York City boroughs of Brooklyn, Queens, and Staten Island. It will also have another indispensable asset – master change agent Robert Catell, chairman and CEO of Brooklyn Union.

Catell is also chairman, president, and CEO of the newly formed KeySpan Energy Corporation. Catell's vision propelled the formation of KeySpan, a holding company that presides over Brooklyn Union and its former subsidiaries, and provides the means for Brooklyn Union to compete in the emerging energy deregulated market.

The Long Island Lighting merger will provide Catell with both the challenge and the opportunity to pursue vital change initiatives on a grander scale. Following the merger, which is going through the inescapable, protracted regulatory screening, Catell will initially be president and COO of the newly merged company, which will provide natural gas and conventionally generated electricity in its core territories as well as operate other energy-related marketing and production businesses. After a year, Catell will graduate to chairman and CEO.

Although he has not dealt with a change management issue of such huge proportions, Catell is prepared to handle this challenge because he is one of the most change-ready executives in American industry, and certainly in the

83

utility field, where he has pushed change while many of his peers have tried to adhere to the status quo.

Catell says he has been living in a change mode for twenty years, since he was a young executive. He spotted the coming changes early on and persuaded, and later led, his company into a variety of preemptive actions. Consequently, Brooklyn Union enters the merger as a total energy company with some very innovative strategies in its approach to the market.

Catell's major focus has been a strengthening of customer relationships, to ensure that its energy users remain with the company when competition begins in earnest. The company enriches these basic linkages with efforts to make sure that its services add value for clients, and that it is tailoring the new services required to meet customer wants and needs.

Another part of the outreach program is to raise Brooklyn Union's visibility in its service area. It is an important sponsor of community events, and programs to foster economic development and job growth. Catell is a role model for his organization through his involvement in many civic organizations. Through his influence, Brooklyn Union has made a major commitment to New York educational institutions.

The internal focus of the culture change has been centered on programs to break the age-old, risk-averse mind-set among the work force. The driving force has been an intense communications and educational program that reaches every employee from "the person reading the meters right up to the top of the company." At the heart of the program, Catell says, is the "willingness of people to accept risk, to not shoot the messenger – all the things that utility companies didn't deal with in the past."

Employee reconditioning is conducted through a wide range of forums – "straight talk" discussion groups in which employees have the opportunity to discuss changes and their implications with Brooklyn Union executives, distribution of literature on key change subjects, and a broad range of formal middle-management education courses developed by university professors.

Catell has personally been a vital contributor, a virtual change agent role model. His visibility and reputation as an executive who makes change happen, rather than just talks about it, have made the communications program more forceful. He has shown himself willing to take risks, over more than two decades as an early detector of change triggers, and as an agent of change in terms of both management and leadership.

As diverse as it was, the entire program has been coordinated around the theme of being "much more of an energy company than just a gas company," Catell says. The formation of KeySpan is a significant step in that change.

Brooklyn Union and its new parent company thus bring into the merger considerable skills in the acquisition and running of diversified energy businesses. The company has entered other energy segments, such as gas marketing, electric services, and oil and gas, and is planning additional acquisitions to expand geographically and industrially.

Change at Brooklyn Union has been facilitated by its commitment to Total Company Alignment, which was unswerving while a variety of initiatives were being pursued. With Catell's oversight, the firm simultaneously revamped culture (encouragement of risk), strategy (diversification into several energy areas), and operations (the right modes and structures to manage multiple businesses). Additionally, compensation systems were realigned to reward those who demonstrated the best performance in areas such as customer service, outreach, and service development.

Although Brooklyn Union is the smaller of the two utilities, its move to KeySpan, coupled with its early change conditioning, should position its considerable corps of change agents – Catell and the change-minded followers he has cultivated – for dealing with the multiple challenges that still lie ahead.

# Betsy Cohen
### Jefferson Bank

Among the giants that dominate Philadelphia banking, Jefferson Bank, with only about $1 billion in assets, will never stand out on the basis of size. Where it does stand out, says Betsy Cohen, founder and chairman, is through a "workable competitive differentiation." That means focusing service on Philadelphia's middle-market business sector and, often, taking contrary positions within the banking industry. But these visible actions grow out of Cohen's unswerving commitment to daily change management as an integral part of the sprightly bank's operating and growth strategy.

Cohen's approach has brought the bank along very well to date. Founded twenty years ago, the bank has seen its growth surge to current asset levels in the last seven years through acquisitions and the creation of services directed to its primary business market. At the very heart of the strategy, she says, is "maintaining a progressive, vibrant workplace," and recruiting and rewarding people who thrive in that environment.

Cohen sees change triggers almost everywhere, and considers herself Jefferson's "orchestra leader" who melds the bank's people and resources to mount appropriate responses and initiatives. Anything from a change in interest rates, to a shift in Jefferson's customer markets, to changes in the law – such as the 1994 congressional revision of federal banking laws – initiates a change trigger that cannot be ignored – and the triggers rarely stop coming.

Agile, nimble people are critical to success under Cohen's baton. She moves people in line with changes in the business, giving them the chance to manage the new lines of business that emerge as the result of change. "I'm looking to give people a distinct opportunity to invest in where they work," she says.

Reward is used to keep employees interested, and to keep them with

Jefferson. "We've grown fast in two decades but we're working on being able to provide significant financial incentives to our employees," she comments. The personnel approach is to combine what Cohen considers the two key elements in driving change-responsive workers – "opportunity and incentive."

Jefferson keeps the culture and reward facets of Total Company Alignment energized by its strategy and mode of operations. "We are a very identifiable locally-based player in the middle market, but to maintain it we have to work twice as hard," she says. Jefferson – which had only $250 million in assets at the close of the 1980s – has implemented this growth plan on a broad front.

There has been attention to growing non-interest income by developing a wide variety of business services tailored for the middle market. The "Smart" line of VISA cards has been launched into consumer markets. Furthermore, the bank has kept up with technological advances in financial services to widen its offerings and reduce its costs.

Acquisitions have been important in expanding Jefferson, led by the purchases of the $100 million Constitution Bank in 1995 and the $125 million United Valley Bank in 1997.

In an era when smaller banks are supposed to fade into oblivion, Jefferson stands out by taking an overtly contrary approach to key decisions. One result is that the bulk of the bank's expansion came amid very difficult economic times. "We invested in a time of contraction," Cohen says. "We hired when the market had good available talent. We acquired branches where it seemed strategically appropriate." Jefferson went against the conventional wisdom, for example, when it invested in the real estate market while that industry was depressed in the early 1990s. "Ours is a long-term view, and one that is supportive of the communities in which we work," Cohen asserts.

The challenge of staying independent could require Cohen and her managerial team to become even more aggressive change managers in the future. It's a challenge she is willing to accept as change triggers continue to buffet the banking industry and competition intensifies. Many larger banks, for instance, have "discovered" the middle market, and Jefferson's strong position among mid-sized businesses won't be impregnable without innovative new products and services that add value for this cost-conscious, relationship-minded group. "Fostering corporate transformation means you don't have to change jobs frequently," she says. "If you're doing it right, you have a new job every year."

Another project is to ensure that change-responsive individuals are functioning as a team, so the little bank can muster its full resources to implement change, and attack the bitterly competitive market. Assembling the change-ready team is not an easy task when the individuals are entrepreneurial self-starters who might feel inhibited by consultation and consensus. Cohen admits to the difficulty of this job but says somebody has to do it. "This is an area of tension for us, but we are aware that it's an area that needs improvement."

Cohen has made a good start by developing a change-ready culture, rewarding and enlarging responsibilities for those who perform under that rubric, and focusing on the importance of growth through specialization. These should be important ingredients in Jefferson's ambitious plans for the future.

# Frances Murphy Draper
## AFRO-American Newspaper Group

In the proper managerial hands, the African-American press represents an intriguing bridge between a legendary, illustrious past and a potentially bright future. That pivotal position demands a highly sophisticated change management initiative to guarantee survival, and at the leading black newspapers, it is being systematically and forcefully practiced by a new generation of executives, many of whom have already won their managerial spurs in mainstream organizations.

A prime example is Frances Murphy Draper, president and COO of the AFRO-American Newspaper Group. Draper is a member of the family who founded the widely respected publishing organization more than one hundred years ago. Using a refreshingly broad-based perspective, Draper regards her company's principal change management challenge as a multifaceted issue that requires a deft balance of internal and external initiatives. The keys to her approach include a more collegial managerial style (in place of the "fairly autocratic" tenor of her family predecessors), constantly upgrading the news coverage of the black community, and reaching out more aggressively to the marketplace.

But the harsh reality is that a high priority must be accorded to selling the advertising, which generates the financial lifeblood of any publishing firm. Although this is often a difficult sale, Draper proudly reports progress in persuading big-ticket advertisers to apportion some of their space and dollars to AFRO-American's products (three weeklies and an electronic edition). The major challenge is getting in to see the advertising person, who is used to dealing primarily with mass mainstream media. On the positive side, once an appointment is made, there is a good prospect of making the sale.

"Most people are reasonable when you get in to see them and show them your product," Draper reports. "They usually respond favorably when information is presented in marketing terms and they are clear about what you are asking them to do." The facts and the business opportunity are all-important, she notes, because the usual "mind-set of the advertiser does not include the African-American weekly in the media mix."

Draper and her salespeople do have a good story to present, which also takes advantage of the shifting trends in the black press that Draper and her modern counterparts are seizing as a clear opportunity. An assemblage of mostly big-city weeklies, the black press of the past was formerly the main (if not the only) source of meaningful news for African-American readers, the champion of equal rights and economic uplift, and strongly stamped with the opinions of its entrepreneurial founders and operators. Today, economic change has created a threat – and the ranks of black weeklies have been shrinking – as mainstream media pay more attention to African-Americans and they, in turn, spend more time with mainstream media.But the well-managed African-American publisher, like Draper's Baltimore-based organization, can nevertheless retain a unique niche as "black community newspapers." This means a potential audience of 12% of the population, which "controls a substantial amount of disposable income as well as the income to purchase necessities." The AFRO-American Group estimates that it reaches 120,000 readers a week, based on its pass-along rate and its 40,900 base circulation.

Why is it that the AFRO-American Group and other black news organizations can produce the kinds of numbers that will make advertisers listen? Once considered anachronistic as racial lines blurred, the survivors in the black press have hung in quite well because they still serve a definite need for African-Americans. Draper and her teammates have astutely blended this combination of sociodemographic and economic developments into strong selling points on their behalf.

Basically, the African-American press presents a balanced coverage of the black community that is skirted by mainstream media. While blacks may be represented in 50% to 60% of the content of a television newscast, "95% is of a negative nature." "We try to balance the coverage in a way that, when you pick up our paper you will see more positive stories than not," she says. "You may see a crime story because that is a fact of life, but you will also see stories that highlight the many successes in the African-American community." She further adds, "We have the opportunity in our newspaper to report things that you won't find in the daily paper."

Catering to the market demand requires a parallel emphasis on news gathering, reporting, and writing, so that the papers are timely and meaningful. Besides pushing standard practices to upgrade coverage, this means recognizing that newspapers are people businesses that must reflect a wide range of disciplines, skills, and interests. Getting all these people to work together is essential, and that initiative represents one of the clearest internal breaks with the autocratic past.

Draper's aim is to capitalize on the vast experience of the veteran managerial corps – some of whom have twenty-five to thirty years of service with the company – while maximizing the talents of the younger people. This has led to what Draper calls a "collaborative kind of planning and brainstorming." Constant dialogue and interchange of ideas are utilized to bridge generational differences, as well as to coordinate the functional arms of editorial, production, advertising, circulation, human resources, and accounting. "When I meet with the advertising sales department, we generally invite people from other departments to the meeting."

The entire operation is designed to allow everyone to contribute to the idea mix. Draper stokes the interchange with "open and honest communications" to develop trust among the workers, who take part in the development of both short-term business tactics and long-pull strategies. But she realistically points out that none of this develops on its own and it must be continually stressed by visible and active top management, with a consistent leadership style. Just going around the work floor and asking people to adapt, without a commensurate effort at the top, "sends the wrong message."

# Herbert Elish
## Weirton Steel Corporation

Herbert Elish, a Harvard-trained lawyer with extraordinarily diverse experience in the executive ranks of both the public and private sectors, takes a long-range view of the execution of change initiatives. He says that the change process should be evolutionary, not revolutionary; gradual, not abrupt; pro-people, not anti-people. Based on that perspective, Elish has to be considered a consummate change manager; his approach is that of a genuinely change-responsive person.

Although Elish's consistent actions on behalf of change haven't generated the lurid headlines reserved for more radical change imperatives, they have quietly but effectively worked. He has used them to help mastermind the highly successful restructuring of International Paper Company, where he was head of human resources; to promote greater efficiency at New York City's Sanitation Department ,where he served as commissioner; and perhaps most notably, as the chairman and change architect of Weirton Steel Corporation, one of the largest employee-controlled corporations in the U.S.

Now retired, Elish says a commitment to gradualism requires the good change agent to be constantly on the lookout for the forces of change and the change triggers they unleash. At best, the alert change agent can detect and project the forces before the triggers actually land any blows. But at minimum, the agent buys the time to plan and choose the most salutary options, and to institute the working parts of the change initiative so they will have the most effect and require the least amount of trial and error.

An Elish-style commitment to constantly monitoring developments with an eye toward inevitable change can be especially rewarding in today's business environment. In Elish's view, business across the world is undergoing a technologically-driven transformation, of a magnitude that recurs perhaps once every 75 to 100 years. One fallout from this leap-frogging technological advancement is the dislocation of people. While Elish hopes that the government will ultimately adopt a policy to ease the pain of this dislocation, he also incorporated humane perspectives into his programs, such as the one he directed at Weirton.

The West Virginia steel company was in the center of myriad forces of change, some moving faster than others. The company's markets were growing modestly, but customers were demanding higher quality and competitive pricing. Technology was producing labor-saving equipment that offered the benefits of increased efficiency, improved productivity, reduced costs, and higher quality – but at the cost of a reduced work force at an employee-controlled company.

Elish ultimately cut the work force from 8,300 in the mid-1980s to about 5,500 a decade later – and did it almost without any pain. Rather than cut from the outset, Weirton put stringent caps on new hires, while it simultaneously invested heavily in a long-range capital investment program to upgrade technology and retire older capacity. Overtime was used extensively to preclude the need for additional personnel. When the new capacity was finally phased in, about 400 jobs were eliminated. But most of the older workers had already retired or were ready to retire. At that point, there was a concerted effort to increase the levels of voluntary retirements with a sweetened retirement program.

"That was fundamentally a combination of what's right and a responsibility to people," Elish comments. He concedes that he was able to go about change in a personally satisfying way because he was lucky enough to have board endorsement, control of the shares by an ESOP that shared his desire for minimizing people injury, union flexibility, and a high ratio of workers nearing retirement. But he believes that many other companies could also practice gradualism and minimize disruption.

This is possible if the change agents are consistently change-responsive in how they look and plan for inevitable change, and is just one of the many approaches to change that may be customized to the individual company under the concept of deengineering.

# Michael Emmi
## Systems & Computer Technology Corporation

When a business is about to go under, the chief executive basically has three options. He can fold his tents and run, clean up the company for a timely sale, or spearhead a fight to increase its value.

Michael Emmi, the CEO of Systems & Computer Technology Corporation, chose to fight – a risky course to be sure, but one that has paid off. And if Emmi hasn't totally shed risk as he implements his ambitious plans for future growth, he has set SCT on a solid foundation from which it can move ahead with considerable confidence.

When he took over the computer and data processing services firm about a decade ago, Emmi could have easily pulled the plug. The company was on the brink of failure. It had a bad reputation in the marketplace. Its image was further scarred when a former CEO was jailed on a securities fraud conviction. But Emmi saw a very definite strength – expertise in client server computing – that could be capitalized on, and which justified taking the risk of trying to resuscitate SCT. Emmi was encouraged to attempt the ultimate in change management challenges because change triggers in the marketplace were increasing the demand for client server computing and offering opportunities for a sharp-eyed company that could customize its services to edge out competitors. "Underneath the covers, SCT's biggest strength was that we were an early adopter of what is called 'client server computing' and that is a very hot market."

Emmi began the recovery effort by emphasizing two main businesses – outsourcing or management of data processing facilities and providing administrative-type software packages. This enabled SCT to offer top-quality data processing services to companies in industries whose needs for electronic on-line information were intensifying but that lacked the skills to handle the operation on their own, or simply didn't want to commit the capital. Now he is in position to expand SCT into systems integration, which involves the organization of large-scale information systems for customers.

While expanding the functional expertise of SCT, Emmi has also plugged hard to find the markets – principally those wracked by major change – that can best use its services. SCT now has the leadership position in higher education, where administrative costs are high and cost-containment has become a major goal, and local government, where efforts to reduce costs often are tempered by political realities. The company is also enjoying rapid growth in the newest of its primary markets, utilities, where the change trigger of deregulation has offered extraordinary opportunities for SCT.

SCT's specialties are customer information and billing systems, which Emmi says are "way out of date for a deregulated environment." SCT actually warmed up by serving the utilities industry in Europe, where deregulation from government control to private ownership started the ball rolling – then shifted to the U.S. where the change is from regulated monopoly to market-based competition.

The results of SCT's evolution from a sick company to a market-focused, change-responsive powerhouse are financially impressive. Revenues are in the $170 million- to $180 million-a-year range and SCT is well in the black, with the financial resources to fuel a growth plan targeted at $500 million a year in revenues in five years.

The initiative is based on a combination of increasing share in existing markets, adding new ones, and developing new skills. For example, Emmi is seeking to buy a firm specializing in administrative software for the manufacturing industry. "The manufacturing software market is the largest packaged software market in the world," he notes. In 1996 alone revenues were $3 billion.

Size presents great opportunities, and seizing a significant new market share would contribute mightily to SCT's growth. But the real opportunity for value-added services comes from the great changes in the industrial sector that put a premium on reduced costs and greater productivity.

Perhaps the biggest challenge facing SCT is staffing. The growth plan calls for expanding the company's complement of technical workers from the present 1,700 to 5,000. "The biggest issue we face is getting the right people at the right cost," Emmi says.

Who are the right people? SCT needs professional and technical workers with skills. But, in addition, the new hires must have the motivation and the change-responsive characteristics that suggest commitment to SCT's growth as well as Emmi's vision of widening share in existing markets and finding new markets and lines of business.

To develop the concept of change-responsive people in specific detail, Emmi has shifted a former marketing vice president to the human resources department. His task is to define the characteristics of the right employee and to sketch the most economical way of recruiting and compensating such people.

Emmi went beyond the human resources department and picked not only an operating executive but one with proximity to the marketplace and an understanding of the people skills needed to retain a competitive edge under the toughest conditions. Perhaps no other area can provide the perspective of day-in, day-out change management as well as sales and marketing, because nimbleness and agility are often the difference between getting and losing a sale.

# Gary Fernandes
## Electronic Data Systems Corporation

If change doesn't find Electronic Data Systems Corporation, it is a certainty that EDS will find change. The former scenario is unlikely in the EDS world of computer technology, where advances and new developments seem to be forged on a daily basis. Yet, EDS takes no chances and relentlessly pushes the envelope itself at every opportunity as an integral feature of its strategy and operating mode.

Gary Fernandes is EDS's vice chairman; he is also a change agent who creates crises from within by crafting difficult problems that his management is challenged to resolve with technical marketing or other innovations. In a sense, these crises are theoretical, but they are all reality-based and may well arise in the marketplace at some point. The payoff in all of this for EDS is that it has a handle on the problem before it actually erupts and can thus craft a solution to its business advantage well ahead of its competitors.

Stealing a march on the competition is critical to survival, Fernandes believes, and the internally manufactured crisis is his primary vehicle for keeping EDS on a course of constant progress. It is also a unique form of anticipatory management that can flower under deengineering, as the company itself devises its own brand of change management.

In EDS's case, Fernandes considers the telescoping of responses to change to be critical because he lives in fear that the company's very success can breed smugness and laziness. Fernandes says,"You have to reinvent yourself while you're going forward."

EDS has literally been reinventing itself for more than a decade, and with Fernandes as its spark plug, the innovations have come in droves. The company reassumed independence in 1996, when it was spun off by General Motors Corporation, its parent for twelve years. But it was now far different from the company that GM acquired in 1984, a batch-oriented data processing operation with developing skills in specialized information services, which H. Ross Perot had founded in the 1960s. By the time it reemerged as a stand-alone concern, EDS had been converted into a provider of value- added systems and solutions that offered demanding clients a premium, higher-margin array of services. In a major post-spin-off move, EDS acquired a management consulting firm, A.T. Kearney Incorporated, that not only expanded its skill base but stamped it as a full-fledged consulting organization. Acquisitions have also been important in spreading EDS abroad, as it copes with the rapid globalization of the industries it serves.

Fernandes occupies an enviable position in pushing change. He is skilled in both the technical and managerial ends of the business, and constantly knits the two together in the belief that a solid infrastructure is needed to fully capitalize on technological breakthroughs. This broad perspective allows him to clearly communicate the company's complex plans, challenges, and change initiatives across a diverse array of disciplines and professions. And it gives him an intriguing hook for practicing Total Company Alignment.

The effort to keep the company balanced occurs on several levels. Strategy and operations are geared to projections of customer demands for information technology, which are determined by intensive market intelligence efforts. People are rewarded for responding and anticipating these market shifts. They are recruited on the basis of their willingness to seek out change, their ability to be challenged and stay on their toes in response to internally manufactured crises, and their skills to capture profitability from a market in a constant state of flux.

Fernandes takes every extra step necessary to make change work for EDS. He fiercely advocates the protection and encouragement of change agents within the organization and works hard to put them in prominent positions. He bemoans the fact that at many companies "the nail that stands out frequently gets hammered." But such people are treasured at EDS, because they form a loyal army of change-minded allies who are dedicated to advancing the company while enhancing its value. The true change agent, he points out, is willing to take on unpleasant tasks, court the displeasure of co-workers who are less enamored of the need for change, and even put their own careers at risk, to promote beneficial innovation.

Thus, a large part of Fernandes' job consists of promoting an environment in which the major engineers of change are supported. When placed in the right positions, sprinkled through all levels of the company, given proper charters and high visibility, they become role models for constant change initiatives. They also serve as communicators between the line and the executive suite to report on how alignment of strategy, operations, culture, and rewards can be maintained as EDS continues on its fast-paced track.

Thanks to his allegiance to the precepts of deengineering, Fernandes has also developed a unique view of teamwork. He favors it when it is a matter of getting everyone in EDS on the same page in support of the need for significant change. That, in turn, leads to the utilization of teams for implementing the programs developed from change initiatives. However, that is where the team idea ends.

EDS banks on individuals, who are steeped in the characteristics of change to monitor the markets for change triggers, to determine their real impact on the company, and to craft an intelligent response to them. These people enjoy vision, imagination, and creativity and are unfettered by the protocols that often govern team-based projects. Their presence is testimony to the fact that a change-responsive organization is only as good as its change-responsive people. A big supporter of the power of the individual in a deengineered environment, Fernandes says, "Only an individual can see around corners. Only an individual can institute a vision."

# Jean-Pierre Garnier
## SmithKline Beecham PLC

Absent a life-threatening crisis from the marketplace, the most convulsive event that can occur in a business organization is a large merger that transforms the company with across-the-board alterations in size, configuration, product mix, and other important dimensions. This is especially true in the case of a merger of equals which creates a third company to succeed both of the former constituents. A common response in such a newly forged concern is to tweak the culture here, to combine the departments there, and sometimes to allow the two partners to continue autonomous operations under a holding company, in the belief that the less done, the less the upset.

Such half-hearted measures were not good enough for SmithKline Beecham PLC, the Anglo-U.S. pharmaceuticals giant, which took the position that to become a new company in name only would destroy the benefits of the merger that created it. Thus, SmithKline daringly decided to sweep away the trappings of its two predecessors and build a totally new organization. It began by instilling an entirely new culture – a "winning culture" – and building principal business drivers, such as research, product development, marketing, and compensation systems around it.

In the words of Jean-Pierre Garnier, Philadelphia-based president and COO of pharmaceuticals and consumer health care, what the company did was "reinvent itself basically from scratch."

London-based SmithKline, by hammering out and implementing its own far-reaching change plan, utilized the freedom engendered by deengineering to create a paradigm – in approach and commitment, if not in specific actions – for the huge company that was being formed to handle the challenges in markets punctuated by constant change triggers.

SmithKline's rejection of change management timidity resulted from several important influences. One was the globalization and technological

100

advances within the pharmaceuticals industry, intensified by the pressure for a continual stream of new products that meet the growing demand for cost containment. Another was the new company's origin in the U.K.'s Beecham PLC and SmithKline Beckman Corporation of the U.S. The merger was aimed at creating a company with the scale and extensive research capability to compete in the global marketplace, but also at propping up two companies with serious gaps in their product lines and technical abilities.

There were deep concerns, Garnier concedes, that retention of the old mores of either company would not support bold plans for the future. "It is easy to define what you want to be, and what your core competencies are," he says. "But if you do not create a winning culture, then you are not going to get strategic alignment from top to bottom."

An aggressive champion of the new culture and the actions that make it live, Garnier is uniquely equipped to oversee one of the most dramatic change management initiatives. French-born and a resident in the U.S., Garnier is a Ph.D. with a broad vision that gives him a grasp not only of the technical and business side of SmithKline but also of what is needed to tie them together. This is evident in his management of an environment, which sets the tone for operations and success while also energizing the culture into an action mode.

In Garnier's view the most visible result is a total change in "the way we discover drugs." The pipeline has gone from a workshop process – one target, one drug at a time – to essentially an assembly-line system in which useful products emerge at a faster rate. Where it formerly took two years to launch a new product and get it into the world's top 10 markets, SmithKline can now do it in three months.

"It costs the same to develop a drug, whether you introduce it in one market or in 60 markets," he asserts. "It is very important to maximize our returns from our new products, and to do that we needed to put in place a transplant system that would allow the marketplace to find exactly how the new product will come out, what it will look like, and what its effects will be, so it can be effectively sold throughout the world. The company that can do that

101

better than others on a global scale will gain maximum advantage."

One bonus from the telescoped discovery process is that a new drug can be introduced in the markets with less-intensive regulation and generate revenues while awaiting approval in the more regulated markets, which have up to a two-year hold on product entry during the screening review. "So we have gained two years of sales," Garnier notes.

In the quest for competitive advantage, the newly developed culture fans out from the laboratories to the marketing and reward elements of the company. The sales force is both a critical instrument for activating the culture, and a primary agent for linking drug discoveries with the market, as well as an exemplar of the reward system. Garnier says the effectiveness of the sales force is measured by how well it captures dominant market share and how well it satisfies its primary customers, which SmithKline says are the physicians who prescribe the drugs.

Markets are determined by geographical niches so each salesperson can be properly assessed as to how he or she fares against competitors selling in the same territories. Feedback is constantly obtained from physicians to determine their views on the efficacy of SmithKline products and whether the company – through its salespeople – has provided effective back-up service and sufficient meaningful information. Sales force compensation is aligned with the quantitative measurement of share and the qualitative measurement of satisfaction, providing a two-pronged incentive for optimal performance. "We feel that the real criterion of compensation is how much better the sales force is than the competition in its respective geographic areas," Garnier states.

Facing a continually evolving market, SmithKline continues to fine-tune its version of Total Company Alignment. But it's hard to top an accomplishment that features a brand-new "winning culture" as the enduring keystone.

# John Georges
## International Paper Company

Anyone who believes that a company in a flat, commodity-oriented industry doesn't have to change is setting up that business for an early death. Some of the biggest success stories in modern business have been written by executives who took old-line companies in mature businesses and recast them as sleek, lean-and-mean tigers, with the ability to perform splendidly by staying ahead of the competition.

One of the most glittering of these achievements was engineered at International Paper Company, once the epitome of the highly integrated muscle- bound company, whose structure was no longer applicable to the conditions in its marketplace. The experience of IP is a clear indication that companies of its ilk are not only worth saving, but can be turned into world-class operations. The primary ingredients are recrafting the company from within, and having a committed change manager at the helm – like John Georges, retired chairman and CEO – who not only drove a massive reorganization over more than a decade but continues to remind the company of the need for new change initiatives.

IP is a classic case of deengineering in that it developed on its own the change management program that best served its needs, led by a consummate apostle of deengineering. The drive behind this approach was that Georges was an extraordinary general manager who was able to bring a diversity of skills and interest to the job and knit them together as a practical timetable for change management.

Most visible to outsiders were the series of strategic moves that IP accomplished – it disassembled many of the vertical integration components that had traditionally dominated the papermaking industry, spent heavily to increase productivity at surviving plants, and widened margins by expanding its product line into higher-margin items (through acquisi-

103

tions – such as writing paper manufacturer Hammermill – and product development).

Behind the actions, however, was an extraordinarily well-thought-out game plan that reflected Georges' wide variety of interests. Synthesized, they were the primary elements of a Total Company Alignment that kept IP on an even keel while it was executing a great shake-up in a company of long tradition. Georges, who began sparking the theme of change in the 1980s, was even able to go beyond his primary areas of expertise by designing a simple, yet effective, compensation system that rewarded his people for getting in front of the change effort.

Georges and his IP colleagues credit much of the success to the development of a relatively formal, highly specific blueprint that set the course for the progress of the initiative. Putting the program on paper was not taken lightly. It had to be definitive enough to communicate goals, but not so hidebound that it would create inflexibility. The blueprint is an all-purpose epistle of the values of well-executed deengineering. For openers, Georges saw the blueprint as a communications tool that spelled out "yearly goals" and outlined "a way of doing things" so that there would be some specificity that could be telegraphed unceasingly to people at all levels of the company. In true deengineering fashion, the blueprint was conceived as a way of identifying the key issues in change management at IP and setting priorities for handling them. As time progressed, new issues were incorporated in the plan. Ultimately, the blueprint was transformed into an action document that served as a benchmark for measuring progress. "Over time, we laid out our major issues and initiatives, like quality, customer service, safety, people development, and product and process development," Georges comments. "We now had a written plan designed to eliminate surprises."

The blueprint is considered the centerpiece of a "built-in change process," since it can be updated with new issues and other matters annually, and the timetable for reaching goals can be set or revised accordingly. Changes come consistently, rationally, and in a systematic manner that IP's people can understand and buy into. That is a critical piece of the Total Company Alignment mosaic, because IP has worked relentlessly to instill a change-responsive culture, no mean feat in a firm traditionally wedded to a staid, commodity operation. Potentially, IP's environment can easily be conducive to great tensions, but Georges is determined to prevent that. "I don't tolerate turf issues," he states. "We've tried to create a culture to run this business. Putting emphasis on key values and institutionalizing those values is what will keep us from divisive internal tensions."

A harmonized compensation program that pays the most rewards to those who actively accept the challenges of change is a finishing touch that both reinforces the change commitment and diverts people from going at each other.

Although the lengthy reorganization has already accomplished much, Georges has kept the change management pot boiling, the blueprint updated, and the change pressures on. He recently transferred the mantle of change leader to his successor, John T. Dillon, who Georges is confident will also serve as a proactive leader. "There can't be any choice on change," Georges asserts. "It won't work for the CEO to be a passive observer of transformation."

The blueprint is essential, because it is a cultural constant in a period when IP continues to press for internal and external change. It allows the company to inherit Georges' change orientation as a linchpin for future action. The cultural effect is important in acquisitions, for example, because it allows IP to quickly merge cultures with a newly purchased target after it has determined that the acquiree is a good match of people, products, and processes. However, IP also recognizes that internal expansion and innovation can be disruptive. So, the blueprint serves the additional purpose of cushioning the inevitable shock waves. "I have looked at it as a way of eliminating corporate bloat and a better way of getting things done across a larger company more quickly," Georges says.

A blueprint of the IP style may not work for everybody, but, as a self-designed and self-revised action plan, for IP's unique situation it has been a masterstroke.

# Rosemarie Greco
## CoreStates Financial Corporation

Change is not an option for the banking industry, says Rosemarie Greco, former president of CoreStates Financial Corporation, and president and CEO of CoreStates – it is an indisputable necessity. In the traditionally hidebound industry, whose foundations are being ceaselessly pounded by gale force winds from every imaginable corner of the world economy, "The banker or institution that stays with the old ways is going to be swept under. Consistent evolution and well-planned, exquisitely implemented evolution is the only sustainable competitive edge."

The most visible manifestations of accelerating change in the industry are mergers and acquisitions, which have created larger institutions, spread them across multiple geographic regions, consolidated the industry, and shrunk the number of banks – while propelling other institutions into new business sectors, and prompting others to narrow operations to their core strengths. These differing effects, Greco points out, are materializing because the industry is being buffeted by so many different types of change triggers, many of them interlocked, which are also causing many other, subtle changes in the way banks operate.

A new-age banker and change initiator, Greco says the trends of globalization, the mushrooming use of technology in financial services, the changing needs of corporate customers, and new demands from the consumer market, cued by evolving career requirements and lifestyles, are some of the most influential drivers of change. In response, modern bankers have had to change not only their product offerings and channels of distribution but their entire mind-set as providers.

The successful bank of the future, Greco maintains, must "reinvent" itself to meet the demands of customers for quick delivery of value-added services in an age of supersonic speed. "Time is the commodity to value,

106

and solutions are what all of us are looking for," she says.

That new environment has led banks to creativity in a number of areas: full-service supermarket-based branches; automated loan centers; the proliferation of automated teller machines; the explosion of debit cards; personal investment services; innovative lending products and services for businesses; and the addition of non-bank financial operations. Beyond these physical changes, there has been a major attitudinal shift, most notably in the treatment of business customers.

Greco believes in the "solution concept": a positioning change from a lending/commodity service approach to a "relationship" arrangement which will actually help consumers manage life event changes and business entities get the benefit of a bank's learning experiences in planning cultural and strategic change management initiatives. "A bank becomes a "partner" for success with customers by thinking through with them solutions for their life and business challenges.

Greco, who worked her way up the ranks from an entry-level job as a secretary, has learned just about every skill needed to do business in the modern era, and expects that she will continually add to her skills. Such requirements have already led bankers away from the traditional business of the industry. Relationships require that the modern banker have the traditional smarts to size up the financial health and business prospects of a borrower but also to know all aspects of the client's business. With a wider horizon, the modern banker must understand how the industry will be affected by legislation or regulation, what leading economic forces are impacting its market, new products, and advancing technologies. These can be used to make an intelligent financing decision and keep the client well-informed.

This approach bridges the line between marketing and financing by increasing its share of business among middle-market companies, businesses that often need the most help to manage change triggers. "The breadth of expertise is important to them as they evolve and mature," Greco points out.

For example, under Greco's stewardship at CoreStates, the bank distributed a software package known as "The Learning Curve", which supplies the families of college-bound students with a plethora of information about higher-education institutions. It can save them huge amounts of time and enable them to bypass costly trips to college campuses for personal inspections.

And at a branch in northwest Philadelphia, CoreStates has created an on-line Personal Investment Center that allows a customer to call up pertinent investment information.

In neither case is there a requirement that the user get a loan, or buy investment services from the bank. However, the college information package is a forceful reminder that the bank offers student loans, and the investment package is a marketing investment, although there is no compulsion to buy through CoreStates. However, Greco notes, "the likelihood of their being predisposed to buy something from us and their thinking of us as a place that cares about them is pretty high."

The modern banker that Greco exemplifies is more interested in continual business development than in maintaining the status quo.

# Paul Grunder
## CPC International Incorporated

CPC International Incorporated is splitting into two parts – spinning off its founding business, commodity-oriented corn wet milling, and keeping its newer but faster-growing branded foods operation. It is another in a series of actions by companies in the U.S. and abroad to dismember the diversified structures into which they evolved, to promote faster growth, and cushion the overall company from continual economic shocks. But the fact that CPC is able to establish corn wet milling as a sound stand-alone operation is attributable to a Herculean change management effort engineered some twenty years ago by master change agent Paul Grunder.

Rescuing the corn wet milling business was not Grunder's only change management feat at CPC, but it was his largest and most glittering success. Based on his track record, his penchant for instituting change, and his willingness to put himself in front of the change initiative, he was the ideal general for the nothing less than top-to-bottom overhaul that was necessary to keep CPC from being drubbed on the battlefield that was the corn wet milling marketplace.

Grunder was handed the baton at a time of tumultuous change in corn wet milling, which CPC had been slow to grasp, and which required nothing less than a quick fix. CPC had become completely misaligned with the realities of the 1970s marketplace, trapped in the past, muscle-bound when maximum nimbleness was demanded. The market had been hit by a multiplicity of change triggers – mergers and consolidation of the customer base which resulted in larger, but fewer, buyers in such user niches as paper, beverages, corrugated boxes, and textiles; outsourcing of technology that previously had been owned by the millers themselves; and increased competition from relatively new entrants like Archer-Daniels-Midland Company and Cargill Incorporated. The business that Grunder inherited was still wedded to a large customer base, competing against the market's traditional players and their heavy investment in technology.

Grunder's counterattack was based on his broad perspective on an industry in flux which enabled him to quickly identify the myriad problems involved, while devising a package of customized initiatives to generate solutions. For Grunder, it was stepping from one change management challenge to another. He had been farmed out to the company's S.B. Penick pharmaceuticals and specialty chemicals subsidiary to realign its business with its unique market requirements. Within two years, he had fashioned the necessary structural renovations; but while Penick's business was going well, corn wet milling was going into a free-fall.

A quick study, Grunder first determined that the change triggers that had destabilized corn wet milling had permanently shifted the business from an "earn" to a "harvest" mode, a movement of tremendous import. Having determined that, Grunder was able to set competitive sales and profit goals for the business and sculpt the most salutary reactions.

He moved on several fronts at the same time. On the personnel scene, Grunder recruited a cadre of change agents and managers, with characteristics similar to his own, and placed them in key positions where they could help lead the charge. This action-oriented corps worked on the company culture, conditioning the work force for transformation into the new operating mode, reinforcing the activities of people considered change-ready, and discouraging opposition from change resistors rooted in the past. To underscore the gravity of the situation, they made visible sacrifices in the name of economy – giving up bonuses, flying coach, sharing secretaries, tightening travel and entertainment expenses. The comprehensive cultural effort was aimed at, and succeeded in, building a reservoir of goodwill.

Communications became an action tool for many phases of the initiative, but was directed principally at getting people through the zone of denial and convincing them that the massive change program was not an overreaction to a temporary upheaval. Measurement, a change driver, was a major adjunct of the communications effort, as the change team cleverly distributed reams of data to show the workers that CPC was no longer competitive in corn wet milling.

With communications orchestrating the cultural conditions, Grunder moved to maximize employee participation, and strengthen buy-in. Managers were directed to perform detailed analyses of competitors' performances and to develop programs for bridging the gaps between their processes and CPC's. Teams were set up to integrate these plans so there would be no internal misalignments, and people were empowered to implement their own ideas. Grunder says, "They were seeking the tie-breaking edge."

Grunder set up the *Thursday* letter, a regular publication that kept everyone abreast of what was going on. It became an important management tool for sharing ideas that were working well.

Organizationally, the corn wet milling business was broken down into smaller units which enabled decisions to be made as close as possible to the marketplace. Grunder stressed that pricing in a commodity business is best handled close to the market, but outside of the sales force, and by an independent management function that can balance all cost decisions with market factors in setting prices. Ultimately, this pricing mechanism was the primary factor in enhancing profitability. When the major change blocks were in place, Grunder drove the business toward two key criteria: making the business competitive with industry leaders on a cost basis and achieving the same return on assets as CPC's Best Foods consumer products operation. That would allow corn wet milling to compete internally for the needed resources. "If you don't get the right level of performance, you won't get the right level of investment," he notes.

Although internal competition for funding will no longer be a factor as the two businesses go their separate ways, Grunder's change principles remain strong points for future management. He believes that change will be driven if the right people are selected, organized properly, and rewarded for self-motivated behavior.

Those concepts need to be prevalent as the corn wet milling business undergoes one of the greatest of all corporate changes, and strikes out on its own. It would do well to embed Grunder's principles in its new charter and strategic plans for future development.

# Leonard Hadley
## Maytag Corporation

Maytag Corporation, the venerable Iowa-based major appliance firm, traditionally considered itself a change-responsive organization. Leveraging a reputation for high quality in clothes washers, dryers, and dishwashers, Maytag looked to the marketplace for ideas on new product development and innovation and internally for the technological advances to deliver on the concepts. That was fine as long as Maytag could thrive by selling a narrow line to the high-price end of the appliance market.

That strategy ended with the massive changes that began to overtake the appliance industry in the late 1970s; Maytag was forced to unleash a change initiative far beyond what it had ever executed in the past. And while the company's history of change-responsiveness did help, it was hardly preparation for the wrenching changes – acquisitions, product expansions, new marketing methods, and so on – that it has endured in the last two decades.

Maytag's current CEO, Leonard Hadley, was actually the executive who first spotted the sea change in the appliance industry, and got the company moving on a strategy to survive it. Hadley took the post of vice president of corporate planning in 1979, when Maytag was a $359 million maker of laundry equipment and dishwashers. He became CEO in 1993, and his only regret is that Maytag did not execute a bolder and faster move a half-decade earlier than his stewardship began. What Hadley discovered in the late 1970s was an industry buffeted by the first wave of a transformation that threatened a well-entrenched niche player like Maytag. "To remain in this game, you had to become a full-line company, serving more than just the high-end market," he comments. That meant selling a wider range of products at a variety of price points. And it was "critical," he notes, that the manufacturer be in a position to provide after-sale service.

What Hadley found was a maturation of the market that slowed growth and made sales volume heavily dependent on the replacement market. Low inflation curbed the company's ability to sustain margins by price increases. The proliferation of "big box" retailers put pressure on manufacturers to deliver large quantities of all types of "white goods" that offered both quality and low price. "Our markets had been saturated by post-war buying," Hadley says. "It got to the point where to gain even incremental market share meant taking share away from one of the rapidly dwindling number of companies left."

When confronted with what had to be done, the change triggers created something of a culture shock at Maytag, for all its commitment to innovation and market-responsiveness. "Maytag," notes Hadley, "had been run by former chief financial officers who were committed to raising the dividend, but did not expand in the marketplace or change the company's strategic orientation."

For Hadley, himself a former financial executive, the strategic findings were a wake-up call. Under his prodding, a strategic planning team developed a widespread acquisition program that added several new appliances – such as ranges, refrigerators and freezers, vacuum cleaners – across a wide price spectrum. By 1986, Maytag had acquired Hardwick, Jenn-Air, and Magic Chef/Admiral, with a resulting five-fold increase in North American sales. Vending equipment firms were later acquired to generate cash flow and counter the earnings cyclicality of appliances. By the late 1980s, Maytag had moved abroad, with acquisitions in Australia and Europe.

"We realized that building a new factory was not an acceptable alternative," Hadley remarks. "Growth through acquisition was what we determined would give the company a good chance of survival."

Hadley, functioning as a change agent to push Maytag into the more extensive operations required by the marketplace, eventually got the job of CEO, where he continues to be challenged by the need for change. For, while Maytag has been in the main successful, its transformation has not been without pain or missteps. For example, there was the need to rationalize Magic Chef/Admiral by closing older plants and shaking up the management, replacing many inherited senior executives. Even more painful was the retreat from Europe, where the acquisition-based expansion simply did not work out.

A key reason for Hadley's accession to the CEO's job was that he has proven his change-responsiveness skills to his peers and – based on the foundation he has created – appears well positioned to look ahead. Through his previous experiences he has learned that change is inevitable and must be countered and looks to gear the "dependability people" for even more agility.

The challenges today are strikingly different. The marketplace is now an arena of competition of giants – five diversified firms control 97% of the appliance volume. But Hadley was a popular choice, because, regardless of what the future holds, he is seen as someone who can steer Maytag in the right direction and who has the sensitivity to realize the trauma in the organization that change creates. Now, true to the credo of the organizational convert, he is so committed to change that change-responsiveness is being imbedded in all parts of the company. For example, executives are being hired for their ability to accept and harness change for the firm's benefit. "What we're looking for in the executives who will lead the company into the next century is the ability to recognize and maximize changes," Hadley says.

# David Holveck
## Centocor Incorporated

It is very difficult to restabilize a money-making company that has temporarily fallen on tough times. However, the difficulty involved in revamping a company that has shown no profits and is still in its formative stages defies measurement.

That worst-case change management scenario was precisely the challenge that was dealt to David Holveck, president and CEO of biotechnology innovator Centocor Incorporated. Had Holveck not succeeded, the former stock market standout would have imploded. But Centocor survives because Holveck, who combines the vision of a scientific dreamer with the hard-nosed fundamentals of a mainstream manager, achieved the seemingly impossible rescue mission. How? By taking the stricken company "back to basics," while mixing speed with a strong dose of care so Centocor could retain the people it needed the most.

Centocor was buffeted by its most overt change trigger when the introduction of the drugs based on its Centoxin compound faltered. But crisis was inevitable, because Centocor's structure, payroll, and operation left it vulnerable to demise. The Centocor that Holveck, a company veteran and former head of the firm's diagnostics division, took charge of in 1993 had too many employees, staggering expenses, and little to show for its efforts.

Although Holveck executed change in several ways, the most visible manifestation of his program was to vastly shrink the size of the company – employment plunged to 500 from 1,600. But Holveck maintains that his approach hardly was haphazard slashing. "Downsizing, if it is done with dispatch, means that you can retain the right people, and work with them, to make the kind of transition that not all businesses get the opportunity to make," Holveck says.

That didn't seem possible when Centocor had its back to the wall after the Centoxin debacle. "This organization was built to support the rapid discovery of several drugs, and on the strong assumption that our flagship compound, Centoxin, would easily pass its second clinical trial," Holveck asserts. "This was a company with an infrastructure burning $20 million a quarter and a drug that cost $4,000 per dose. To break even, we would have needed sales of at least $300 million. When our filing was rejected, everything came unglued. The possibility that we might fail and need an exit strategy was never factored into the organizational equation, even as the remotest possibility."

Holveck, whose qualifications for spearheading change at a company on the brink of becoming a business casualty included management of one of the few successful areas at Centocor, had to erect a new structure that was both scientifically and cost effective. This called for the alignment of costs and skills – which Holveck achieved by concentrating on Centocor's strengths and core competencies. "We had to trim the company without losing the people and the skill sets we needed to regroup," Holveck notes. "The game plan was to measure our progress on cash burn per quarter. The goal was to reduce the burn rate from $20 million to $5 million each quarter. The cash management tightening was not to slow down operations – in fact, it was twinned with a strategy of increasing clinical trials, so new drugs would start generating revenues and the entire company could reach profitability by 1995."

One part of the rescue program was to take in a partner, Eli Lilly, for the continuing development of Centoxin, which was still a promising drug. The partnership was woven into the change management program. "We had to make the choice of which of our core competencies to retain in this partnership," Holveck states. "The marketing, sales, and R&D functions were all fully integrated into the partnership. Functions such as manufacturing and our successful diagnostics business were, at the time, what we were best at. It was on those strengths that I designed the plan to make the company what it is today."

The "back to basics" drive in the main company focused on "staffing limited to the essential groups that had originally built the company, like clinical research and development, manufacturing, and the staff that supported the successful diagnostics business."

Delicacy was a prime influence. "Without it," says Holveck, "you can cut the heart out of an organization." In recognition that the revamping would be painful, Holveck also launched an intensive communications drive to "recruit" Centocor survivors to the needed changes. "We had to tell them what we were planning to do, what elements were key to that plan, and show them how they fit into the plan," Holveck asserts. "And we had to keep communicating with them, describing goals and objectives, and our progress in reaching them." The approach to retaining employee confidence was to offer each person a one-year contract that included the reward system in the change alignment. At the end of that year, Holveck explains, they would either still have jobs or be given adequate compensation for supporting the company during the transition. Since the peak of the change program, Centocor has forged considerable progress and has generally moved along the lines sketched by Holveck's game plan.

Holveck made the best out of a dire situation. He not only kept Centocor afloat but seized the opportunity to point the company toward a new direction. He considers the reorganization "an excellent opportunity to refocus and reshape."

# D on Mabe
## Perdue Farms Incorporated

Perdue Farms Incorporated is living, thriving testimony to the deengineering precept that when the stakes are the highest, major change has to be executed in a total package that sweeps fresh air into all segments of the company at once. When Perdue's back was to the wall because of an abrupt 1970s shift in its marketplace, the Maryland-based chicken grower correctly chose to fight back by undertaking an ambitious change response. Ultimately, it was the commitment to Total Company Alignment that helped the privately-owned business succeed handsomely in a treacherously competitive environment.

Perdue's most direct goal was to push the company up the value chain from chicken raising to processing and marketing. That was hard enough, because Perdue lacked experience in the upstream segments of the business. But to concentrate on the purely physical side of a diversifying change would have meant altering strategy and operations in a vacuum. The company's top management decided that was not enough, and that it would have to be accompanied by a reward system that paid people for performing in a rapidly changing scene and a revamped culture that dramatized the reasons for change. The new culture, in fact, was a centerpiece of the entire change, even though the physical expansion was the most visible result.

In many respects, the decision to rely heavily on a communications-based culture change should not have been surprising, given the nature of the company's top two leaders. The most famous of the two was Frank Perdue, chief stockholder and scion of the family that founded and managed Perdue. Perdue has been an advocate for quality, which he forcefully communicated to the work force during his many years with the company. Responsible for making the company run internally was Don Mabe, who had an unabashed passion for the chicken business and would do anything to hang on as a fierce competitor. Both enjoyed strong credentials with the work force because they were visible managers who bluntly communicated their attitudes to all levels. They proved to be the company's primary assets in driving the wrenching change that was to come and, which, as company executives frankly recount, was hardly seamless.

Historically, Perdue was a primary exponent of a business trend that in the 1990s is known as "outsourcing." It raised poultry for sale to other companies, which processed the fowl, and branded and marketed it. Yet, by the 1970s, although Perdue had not yet been doing poorly, it determined that this narrowly-centered supply operation had a limited life. The big money was being made by forward-integrated competitors, who could promote maximum productivity at low cost to meet the demands of large-volume supermarkets for huge quantities of brand-name chickens and turkeys, delivered in timely fashion, and priced at the lowest possible level. Complicating the problems were that many of the integrated producers who were sewing up the supermarket business were larger than Perdue, and had far more experience in processing and the other elements of integration. The real threat to Perdue was that it could have been entirely squeezed out, because there might not have been a great need for another unbranded supplier.

The prime characteristics of Mabe and Perdue, coupled with their extraordinary grasp of the poultry business, enabled them to move quickly through the several aspects of Total Company Alignment. Perdue's obsession with quality was a rallying force for all employees, and the steady hand that assured that the change initiative would be done right. Mabe supplied the managerial skills to build other TCA elements around the quality theme and through his enthusiasm served as the salesman of change. These contributions were indispensable as Perdue expanded, took on armies of new people, and pushed deeper and deeper into unfamiliar territory.

The well-known advertising program in which Frank Perdue appeared as the company's spokesman was in fact the outgrowth of the total change initiative. His appearances in television spots were designed to first introduce, and later reinforce, the commitment to consumer quality and to simultaneously deliver the same message to insiders, whether they were Perdue veterans or new hires.

The outreach of these two key executives bonded the entire change initiative, when the great volatility involved in the project could have ruptured the company at the seams. There was, for example, the rapid pace of the program, which led to thousands of new workers – ranging from managers with processing experience to lower-level workers charged with manning the newly established production lines. A company that had historically managed a complement of 1,500 workers now had to handle many more. "After we expanded our business, we doubled in size," Mabe recalls. "In four years we tripled our number of employees."

Mabe responded by establishing a human resources department capable of dealing with a larger and more diverse work force. He instituted a benchmarking program, since Perdue was now competing against firms with far more experience in integrated operations. He instituted a formal quality assurance program – a natural for a company steeped in quality – and backed it with compensation incentives for workers who met the standards. He created measurement systems up and down the line. "We have the kind of people who want to be good, and they believe in what they're doing," Mabe says. "The QA process was helpful and confirmed for us that we were as good as we thought we were."

When worker buy-in is a two-way street – when performance is aimed at productive, efficient, and super-competitive operations, and rewards are based squarely on that input – a changing company has done the most thorough job of restabilizing itself. Perdue had a huge asset in the forceful leadership of Frank Perdue and Don Mabe. The company was wise to engineer an awesome change by basing a total program on their impressive managerial styles.

# R. James Macaleer
## Shared Medical Systems Corporation

Shared Medical Systems Corporation was born through a "convergence of industries," in the words of its chairman and co-founder, R. James Macaleer. That's another way of saying that SMS was a product of change. The company, which provides a top-to-bottom array of data processing services and functions for hospitals, not only has had to live through constant change in its twenty-six years of existence but now faces perhaps the most wrenching change of all, as its targeted industry consolidates and there are fewer customers to serve.

SMS is poised to take advantage of the latest change trigger in the hospital market. "There are fewer customers but they are bigger," says Macaleer. "Because of consolidation, they have new software needs. So, it's really a net plus for us."

The company was created as a vital connecting point between the hospital and the computer industries. On one side were the hospitals, buying newly developed computer hardware as their recordkeeping and financial management needs mounted; on the other side were the computer companies selling them the hardware. What was missing was good software that would enable the hospitals to really use the hardware. SMS, started by three IBM salesmen, rushed in to fill the gap by, in Macaleer's words, "taking what IBM had and making it work."

Over time SMS has evolved into a multifaceted business. Not only does it provide the remote processing portion of the business it was founded on but also provides in-house and turnkey computing options, as well as formal outsourcing contracts whereby SMS takes full responsibility for running hospitals' information systems departments. SMS also provides a full range of services – from designing and installing systems, to planning and engineering complex networks and interfaces, to providing a full range

121

of consulting services.

Keeping some critical elements constant is what has enabled SMS to weather the storms of change. For example, it has focused exclusively on hospital customers. "We know the business," Macaleer says, adding that the company's top four competitors are also hospital specialists in the $3 to $5 billion market for providing data processing services to that industry.

Equally important is that SMS remains market-driven. While it is the only provider of off-site processing, it has lots of competition for other services, and tries to beat it back by "outselling them," Macaleer notes. With increased market share serving as a key to growth, SMS "sells solutions, not products" and works at "adding value to its customers."

"We'll put in standard systems," he says. "We'll integrate them. We'll make sure they don't go down. We'll make sure they talk to each other, and we'll solve customers' problems that way." The foundation for this deft mixture of marketing and computer skills is getting "smart people," motivating them, setting goals, and executing objective performance evaluations. That provides an organizational strength that Macaleer credits as "the reason why we have survived and are strong across the spectrum."

Macaleer says SMS' ability to change is also a reason why it has survived. Most recently, the company restructured its organization in response to market needs, the changing customer base, and aggressive competition. It realigned its business units and management structure to achieve greater efficiency and better serve the needs of its customers. But, in a company that has continually made market-driven change, Macaleer says, "It's just business as usual. We try to emphasize to our people that they should not be distracted by changes in the organization. If we lose productivity because of a change, even temporarily, we have failed to meet our objective."

# James E. Marley
## AMP Incorporated

James E. Marley, the chairman of AMP Incorporated, has built his career around the art of being a change master. Whether in his present position, or in lower-level posts, Marley has always exuded and practiced the traits of alertness, decisiveness, and change-responsiveness to the ultimate degree, along with the people-oriented knack of communicating throughout the organization the importance of change and the need to manage it.

Executives like Marley are critical to organizations like AMP, the premier manufacturer of electronic connectors and related products, because change is a constant in their markets. Either the primary players create changes themselves, through new products and technical advances, or the market, usually in the form of the customer base, will thrust change on them, by varying key factors of demand. In that environment, the most successful competitors are those who combine the foresightedness of innovation with the fundamentals of keeping the company together during the periods of the most sweeping change. Marley fills the bill quite well, as evidenced by his leadership in mounting a counterattack against the incredible array of change triggers that have buffeted the connector industry over the last decade-and-a-half.

Remarkably, it took extraordinary skills and measures to keep AMP competitive despite its record of change adaptability. Marley was vice president of operations when the changes began to engulf AMP in the 1980s, threatening its superb record of growth, performance, and technical excellence.

Always on the lookout for change, Marley found it in excess in the last decade. At the same time, the connector industry was inundated with oversupply; was unable to recover development costs through price increases; was hocked by the failure of an expected demand surge from the office equipment, personal computer, and software markets; had witnessed the shrinking of markets and production overseas; and had to respond to increasing demands for product quality.

As Marley saw it, the biggest problem was convincing a company already responsive to change that even more massive change was ahead, and to thus get buy-in for a program far more radical than anything AMP had launched in the past.

That meant nothing less than shaking up the culture – moving from the acceptance of relatively modest change to change bordering on the radical. But true to his change-responsive commitment, Marley realized that jolting the culture alone would not do the job, and that environmental retuning had to be accomplished with concurrent changes in strategy, operations, and rewards. AMP needed an across-the-board effort that stressed stability through the balancing principle of Total Company Alignment.

It was time and effort well spent, for the results were sweeping. AMP closed thirty plants and cut its work force by 25%. It strengthened its strategy as a customer-driven organization by narrowing its focus to three key customer groups – automotive, capital goods, and aerospace. In turn, the operations of each of these businesses were tied more closely to the customer, with quality of product, service, and reduced lead and delivery times established as the primary measures of performance. In a deft interconnecting touch, these criteria also comprised the key benchmarks for compensation and reward.

The cultural aspect was further refined by the installation of truly change-responsive people. Managerial assignments went to people who would achieve product, service, and delivery goals and then would be appropriately compensated for them. But still higher managers were given posts that charged them with responsibility for managing the change-driven operations to an optimal degree. That served to create an almost ideal management structure for the change-minded organization, in which a broad range of supervisors are brought very close to the market.

Tying all of these parallel efforts together were the communications programs crafted by Marley both to emphasize the importance of change and to dramatize the consequences of failing to counter them smartly. For example,

Marley realistically assessed that even a change-minded company like AMP had some change resistors, and his messages let them know that their ways had to change, for their own survival as well as the company's.

"We came up with a three-pronged approach," Marley states. "First, we made it clear that change was embraced at the senior levels of the organization – we legitimized transformation. Second, while it may sound harsh, we made it clear that if you did not share those values, you would be best off at a company other than AMP. Last, we gave continual reinforcement to support change managers in key positions."

Since then, Marley has continued to practice those approaches at AMP, with full awareness that a critical situation like the one in the 1980s could well recur. The AMP of the late 1990s is a much leaner, more focused organization that continues to innovate and lead in its constantly changing markets. And it continues to practice the concept of Total Company Alignment with the balance of its key components, and to bring in people who are committed to the principles of change management.

Most importantly, AMP wrote its own technique for revamping the company to meet the challenges of change, because it was in the best position to determine where it had to go, based on its expert knowledge of its marketplace. It moved swiftly and decisively, freed from the fetters of conceptual complication. AMP was a true exponent of deengineering.

# Gary Mecklenburg
## Northwestern Memorial Hospital

Caught in the pincer of mounting costs and reduced insurance reimbursements, a major non-profit hospital has fought back in a way that more closely resembles the initiative of a profit-making manufacturing or financial services company. At Chicago's Northwestern Memorial Hospital, there is an emphasis not only on reducing costs but on rewarding those managers who save the most.

That is one plank, albeit a critical one, in an ambitious plan crafted by Gary Mecklenburg, president and CEO. Mecklenburg, of necessity a consummate change master, has virtually written the paradigm of change management for the not-for-profit sector. He has gone where no other non-profit chieftain has gone before, effectively using the carte blanche of deengineering to create a survival strategy that includes a non-profit format of Total Company Alignment, recasting the staff as a "learning organization," and instilling a permanently change-ready mentality.

A stickler for efficiency and quality service, Mecklenburg drove Northwestern Memorial into a dramatically new mode, only partially because of the harsh economic realities. Also contributing to his forceful change management initiative was a classic corps of change buffers and resistors who simply would not recognize that the institution was being convulsed by shock waves. Mecklenburg admits to being puzzled by the number of people that "tend to be oblivious to what's going on around them."

Even more perplexing was that these visible, powerful, and upsetting forces of change were creating a "transfer of risk" in the way hospitals are paid. Hospitals traditionally have been compensated on a cost-plus basis, but in this era of the drive for lower health care costs, the old system has been replaced by a melange of insurance, managed care, and other arrangements. The bottom line is that reimbursements are "heavily discounted," and the hospital that avoids cutting costs will face an exacerbated financial squeeze.

Mecklenburg fought back with a wide program designed to make Northwestern Memorial more efficient by reorganizing and reducing management, cutting operating costs, keeping customers and their financial contributions coming, and enhancing the hospital's appeal with improved quality. Many of the steps, including paying incentives to managers who do the most cost-efficient jobs, were devised as reinforcements for communicating the need to keep atop change. "The first step in our organization is to constantly be aware of the change that is going on so we can hopefully stay ahead of the change curve, to anticipate change rather than to react to it," he says.

A "learning organization," to which the theme of change is constantly trumpeted, is the antithesis of the lumbering bureaucratic non-profit organization. Some of its visible trappings have included the creation and implementation of a clear organizational structure with top-notch talent, the installation of superb systems to support them, incisive financial analysis, and a sound strategic plan. The glue that binds these elements together is the "right skills" to "do the jobs that are front of you."

Thus, the "learning organization" is one based on Total Company Alignment, which ties strategy, operational efficiency, compensation based on that efficiency, and reinforcement of harmonized change culture into one neat package.

"In about five years, we greatly streamlined the management organization, by taking out about 50% of the management positions," Mecklenburg says. "As a result, many people who were part-time managers while pursuing full-time jobs as nurses and technicians were taken off the managerial rolls and assigned to their primary practices in delivering patient care." "We also recognized that management is a full-time, valuable role," he says. "Trying to be a skilled manager and a superb clinician at the same time is very difficult."

While changing the personnel landscape, Mecklenburg made it more effective by providing all employees with clear statements of their goals so they would fully understand their new status and assignments. The thrust of the first phase was to improve patient care; it not only succeeded in improving quality but also resulted in a welcome 25% reduction in cost-per-case over the last three years. These twin achievements were managed, Mecklenburg believes, because Northwestern Memorial sharpened the focus of its health care professionals, clearly enunciated their goals, told them they would be evaluated on the basis of those goals, and assigned permanent, skilled managers to handle full-time managerial functions.

Imaginatively and deftly, Northwestern Memorial utilized the fundamentals of for-profit change initiatives, adapted to its own situation, to combat a crisis that could have overwhelmed a less resilient organization.

Northwestern's strategic plan also provides a platform for future operations, where future fine-tuning of change initiatives can be added. It is a primary management tool that encompasses business plans, goals, objectives, tactics, and compensation measures – in effect, the TCA of the future. Compensation, for example, is keyed to the accomplishment of the goals contained in the strategic plan.

A commitment to "learning" and to communications needed to deliver that knowledge are the basis of the entire change process. They stress the reasons for change in unambiguous terms through a variety of media – seminars led by outside speakers, monthly meetings of middle managers, the annual meeting of all 4,000 Northwestern Memorial employees, and so on. "People can deal with change if you give them the information," Mecklenburg insists.

Northwestern Memorial, fighting back at the right time and continuing along the path blazed by true change-ready organizations, remains one of the nation's most respected and successful teaching hospitals.

# Barbara Roberts
## FPG International Corporation

When she was installed in 1990 as president of FPG, one of the world's largest photographic agencies, Barbara Roberts knew there had to be a better way to run the business. She wasn't quite sure what that was – she confesses to knowing little about photography – but she was eager to learn quickly and to get the company up to speed as fast as possible. There aren't many businesses like FPG, which has only a handful of competitors, but to Roberts it seemed to have all the signs of a classically under-managed operation.

If Roberts wasn't steeped in the fine points of photography or the relationship of FPG to its clientele, she was a quick study with an outsider's perspective, and managerial skills honed in key positions in investment banking and direct marketing. She also had a strong ambition to use her business expertise to spearhead a vast improvement in a business that needed help. If the FPG of today bears little resemblance to the agency that began the decade, it is as much the result of Roberts' ability to expand the rigid mind-set of its work force as the actual innovations in operations and technology that she introduced – far-reaching though they may be.

FPG's business is providing photographs from a vast company-maintained bank – "images" of which there are more than 6 million in stock – to a demanding customer base. FPG photos can be ordered by corporate communications departments, advertising agencies, printers, magazines and other publications, greeting card companies, or any form of media needing just the right artwork to make a graphic presentation.

Competitive pressures in this highly specialized field are ever-intensifying, as are the persistent need to modernize technology in line with the customer base. When Roberts came on board, FPG sorely required revamping. Fifty-four years old, FPG was sleepy, old-fashioned, and stagnating under the family survivors of its founder. Stock paper photographs were still being plucked by hand from file cabinets and shipped to customers by mail. Billing and collection procedures were from the Dark Ages. Marketing was virtually nonexistent, and there was little systematic effort to upgrade or expand the files.

Ironically, FPG had managed to limp along because its two primary competitors were also mired in antiquated operations. This led to a rather bizarre situation, which Roberts turned to FPG's advantage – almost the driving force of her total restructuring of the company. The carry-over from that strange setting, Roberts says, was that "in this business you don't get a second chance." In other words, if you fail the customer once, he or she will never return. That began when customers were so dissatisfied with the three major agencies that they got into the habit of calling them all, at the same time, to make sure they would get what they needed. Customers would then return to the agency that was consistently able to deliver. Today, FPG can deliver from a position of strength; it can stress shipping the best photograph "the same day anyone in the United States calls." "If a competitor beats us, we've lost that sale forever," Roberts asserts.

The company is able to meet the demand for speed and quality because its photos are now digitally stored, electronically retrieved, and shipped over a network rather than by mail. It is able to meet customer demand for innovation and freshness in graphics because it retains a stable of 200 freelance photographers who contribute to its expanded file of images. A variety of shots can now be put on a CD-ROM for the client to download and select from for a specific graphics project. Billing and collection systems have been automated, and FPG operates a tough enforcement program to collect the fees for unauthorized use of its photos or for abuse of the licences it grants to high-volume clients for the use of its shots.

Financially, FPG sales have burgeoned – from a few million dollars in 1990 to $40 million in 1997 – and Roberts has ambitious plans to promote even faster growth through intensified and more technical advancement.

Despite the makeover of FPG, at the outset, Roberts' conversion plans weren't exactly met with universal acclaim. The work force was a mix of different types – a quarter of whom, mostly in pivotal positions, were enthusiastic and ready to be change facilitators, but the largest bloc was wedded to the old days and functioned as change resistors. Roberts' task – which she recognized early on – was to accentuate the former and win over the recalcitrants, even though there was across-the-board skepticism that anything would be accomplished.

With a free hand from the company's family owners, and a resolve strengthened by her commitment to principles of deengineering, Roberts began with small, but visible, steps that built on each other to gain change momentum. She launched a quick survey of workers to field their ideas for improvements and quickly put the most useful of them into effect – executing no less than thirty ideas within forty-eight hours. Most were relatively simple and inexpensive – a bulletin board, a refrigerator where employees could keep their lunches. But the alacrity of their implementation, and the sheer number of changes, sent the message that FPG was in a new mode. "This was a company where nothing had happened for fifty years," she remarks. "Right there was a message – call Barbara, give her some ideas. She will respond, and things are going to happen."

Its wider marketplace recognition is a primary example of FPG's new star status. Roberts is extremely pleased that photographic and systems equipment manufacturers continually tap FPG to try out their new offerings and "get our stamp of approval because of our reputation."

While these relationships allow FPG to get first knowledge of the latest technology, Roberts complements that strength with more aggressive marketing, to plug into growth opportunities in cable television, direct marketing and specialty magazines, and programs to expand and add diversity to the images file. For example, shots of Latinos and other minorities and of senior citizens are in high demand but relatively short supply these days.

The future in the business where you don't get a "second chance" is also pegged to proactively reaching customers and listening to their ideas for change. "The secret there is to be very people-oriented," Roberts says.

*FPG International was sold in June 1997.*
*Barbara Roberts is currently on another assignment.*

# Stanley Silverman
## PQ Corporation

Not long ago, PQ Corporation had to plan how to widen distribution of a chemical product manufactured at its California plant which required moving it into rail cars for shipment to the East. The cost of the plant renovations required to facilitate rail loading was estimated by the company's engineers at $500,000. PQ was able to get the project completed for only $65,000 by activating an existing, but unused, conveyor system.

At another PQ facility, plant personnel and a key customer were not communicating about the specifications for a product. The plant manager and a group of production people visited the customer's operation, came to an agreement on the customer's specifications, and developed a higher-performing product that was exactly what the customer wanted.

In still another instance, PQ faced a thorny problem because one of its products did not flow as well as competitors' products when it was used by manufacturing customers. The solution came from a multidisciplinary team that analyzed the problem and redesigned PQ's production so that its product would be easier to use.

What do these three anecdotes have in common? In each case, hourly workers were heavily involved. In California, the idea for using the existing conveyor system came from a shipping department employee; in the other cases, production workers played a large role in solving the problems.

This unusual degree of input from the shop floor was neither accidental nor isolated but an anticipated objective of PQ's remarkable change management program begun in 1989 with the working title of "Continuous Quality Improvement" (CQI). The main value driver in CQI is the delivery of customer satisfaction at all levels of the company, but getting to that goal has prompted an unswerving commitment to Total Company Alignment.

132

The prodigious contributions from the shop floor mean that CQI is paying off, according to Stanley W. Silverman, executive vice president and COO, who helped design the program and has remained an unabashed salesman for its full implementation. "The real strength of the company is the people on the factory floor," Silverman asserts. "Our job is to give them the resources to work with so they can do their jobs."

The development and execution of CQI mirrored PQ's massive two-decade transformation from a smallish North American commodity chemicals producer with $30 million in sales to a diversified global organization, which now owns seventy plants in twenty-one countries and whose sales volume now approaches $500 million. The old style had to go, and its replacement had to recognize not only the international sprawl and product diversity but also that the privately-owned company would continue to remain in an "earn" or growth mode. As CQI developed, it worked to muster all PQ resources to meet the challenges of operating in globalized markets with intensified competition and changing customer requirements. Productivity became increasingly critical, customer satisfaction a powerful competitive weapon, and top-to-bottom participation both the primary operating style and the core of its corporate culture.

For starters, PQ handled the structural part of TCA by melding a group of small independent regional units into an integrated worldwide network, built around three global businesses set up to cover markets, facilitate technology transfer, and maximize synergies. As the physical configurations were hammered out, PQ was in the process of overhauling the company culture and corporate philosophy based on "open and free communications between all levels within the organization," Silverman says. That means that lower-level workers were invited, indeed encouraged, to disagree with their bosses, and that when they did, the bosses had better listen. "We don't want a bunch of executives or managers who won't take advice from the lower levels. We have empowered the lowest levels of the organization to be full participants and have an influence in the business."

PQ takes myriad steps to support the culture, including a panoply of events such as "town meetings" at company plants, where executives meet with other personnel, and a worldwide "fair," at which people who have helped institute changes at company facilities – ranging from incremental modifications in production processes to technical breakthroughs – display their accomplishments. In addition, the PQ approach leaves lots of room in both culture and organization for change agents at what Silverman calls "the edge." "At the edge, we want people to try a lot of things that are brand-new," he comments. "There is a lot of turbulence along the edges where we look for the state-of-the-art in our areas of expertise. We want people to be able to benchmark – both internally and externally – for best practice. We want agents of change along the sides."

Encouragement of change agents who will assume responsible risks, says Silverman, is PQ's way of countering the zone of self-deception, which has trapped so many companies, and required them to undertake "a Herculean effort to get back to where the market was." It's also part of keeping the entire company flexible so that it can take change in stride. "They do wild and crazy things at the edge – these change agents," he states.

But the principal reinforcement for the culture of total company buy-in and combined operations is that PQ is willing to pay to make it work, and employees are willing to go for the carrot. A revamped compensation system rewards workers for achievements and eliminates one of Silverman's pet peeves – what he calls the "zero-sum game." It's zero-sum, he says, when the company decides on an average pay hike for all workers, then rewards the best performers more generous increases but scales back the pay boosts for poorer performers. The PQ system rates all employees on a scale of 100 – with "good" performers carrying a rating of 50 or better, and "exceptional" performance meriting 67 or better. The performance also has to be sustained over a period of time to merit the highest rewards. The actual compensation is scaled to the sustained performance ratings. "This approach," Silverman says, "nullifies competition between employees for the biggest pay boosts and promotes unit or department teamwork to push for peak results. Everyone on the team gets rewarded and they are not competing for salary dollars." In fact, PQ has found that frequently the money paid out in dollars actually exceeds the "structure movement" set by the company. But "with the performance we get out of it, who cares?"

# Toshiaki Urushisako
## Sharp Corporation

Sharp Corporation, the Japan-based electronics giant, manages constant change on several levels. It is a technological innovator, creating change for itself and for a large group of other companies that include competitors, customers, and suppliers. It is always on the move geographically. It is constantly entering all kinds of new markets – by product, function, geography. In all of these ways, Sharp maintains a ceaseless commitment to change management and utilizes a unique organizational structure as the mainstay of this effort.

Summing up the utility of its unified structure, Toshiaki Urushisako, chairman of Sharp Electronics Corporation, Sharp's U.S. subsidiary, based in Mahwah, New Jersey, puts it this way: "It's important to maintain the closest possible contacts with the markets. Organizationally flat, flexible structures supported by business-focused informational support are crucial to providing flexible responses to unforeseen situations."

Sharp's structure is no mere artifact. It provides a fundamental framework for supporting growth and innovation with mechanisms that reach out into the marketplace, keeps the drumbeat of change pulsing through its personnel in many countries, and unites key operating elements. Urushisako says the structure provides a common roof for everything, from well-financed research and development, to highly efficient production, to the continual internal adjustments that promote organizational and operating balance in the face of change.

The flat organization promotes the desired qualities needed for a total commitment to change. "The structure allows us to significantly broaden the support of our markets through controlled decentralization, and without significant impact on overall staffing." The organizational design, therefore, is simultaneously an instrument of change and a structure that can cushion the impact of change triggers. The primary consideration then becomes the most effective way of dealing with change, rather than the fear of being penalized by change. In addition, the organization becomes the linchpin for full implementation of Total Company Alignment.

"Each organization must adapt the elements of management that best fit its corporate culture." These features must be buttressed by effective leadership, directed toward building and communicating a vision of the corporate future and sketching *broad paths* for achieving it. Communication leading to total buy-in is vital. "This vision must be *sold to* and *bought by* the rest of the organization, and a broad consensus must be developed around it," says Urushisako. "The keys to this process are the selection of the appropriate management staff, and the ability to communicate with all elements of the operation." Organizational structure then becomes a vehicle for promoting change through a variety of functions, rather than an end in itself. It becomes a power station for communicating ideas to the work force, reaching into the marketplace, and getting a full commitment to market alignment with a platform for fine-tuning when necessary.

Sharp has its eyes set on the future and intends to shape it through its technological prowess. "Technological changes will cause the planet's entire social mechanism, ranging from business operations to consumer life-styles and leisure patterns, to drastically change," Urushisako asserts. If this viewpoint suggests that change may be even more rapid and sweeping than in the past, Urushisako says that Sharp is girding itself for that eventuality. Many of the projected outcomes have been incorporated into present operations, including intensive product planning to meet marketplace needs, close contact with distribution channels to monitor their patterns of change, and hefty investment of money in research and development and capital spending.

In sum, all these branches on the organizational tree link innovation, production, market contact, and complete flexibility. The organization then serves as a metaphor for Sharp's individual brand of deengineering.

"We focus on producing new 'cutting-edge' devices and demand-producing products on these new technologies," the Sharp executive says. "In this competitive environment, products that generate new demand are absolutely critical for current and future growth."

# L eslie Vadasz
## Intel Corporation

Among the most admired and closely watched companies in the world is Intel Corporation, the premier producer of microprocessors for personal computers. Whether measured by growth, performance, technical innovation, or new products, Intel perennially emerges as the king of the hill in demanding and ceaselessly changing market segments. But uneasy sits the head that wears a crown – and Intel itself is the primary contributor to its insecurity. "You won't find a more paranoid company," says Leslie Vadasz, senior vice president.

Vadasz is an exemplar of the mentality shared by Intel management which is driven by change and the obsession to stay ahead in a market segment that presents not only enormous growth prospects if the status quo is not disturbed but even greater opportunities for reward by capitalizing on change.

As with many change challenges, Intel's is unique, as natural and innovation-based growth trends are running in tandem and require a unique brand of systematic response. Intel seeks to meet its challenges and stay in front of the market segment with a program that eschews the "not invented here" syndrome. As Vadasz notes, Intel not only practices the change game on its own but spurs a wide range of associated companies to adjust simultaneously.

Vadasz states that it is a fact of life in the computer industry "that there are many constituents to a market segment." No one firm can supply all the needs of computer and information systems. Thus, when one key supplier of components has to make an adjustment, many more have to change. A firm like Intel is as much concerned with its individual change initiative as with setting a clear example for others. Alignment to a market segment, critical in operating success, depends not just on Intel's efforts but on a multitude of companies with a sweeping variety of disciplines and perspectives.

Equipped with such advantages as its market segment positions, unsurpassed technological know-how, and financial resources, Intel is in a rare position to set the pace. It pursues its goals by providing technology and information to others, offering education forums for computer makers and their end-users, and even by investing in companies, providing capital for accelerating technological advances. As a hub in this strategic arena, Intel, by design and by result, effectively thumps the drumbeat of change both within its own ranks and outside.

Vadasz is among the growing corps of late 20th Century leaders who emphasize the need to simultaneously drive change both internally and externally. This contingent is characterized by its willingness to take risks, assume leadership, and to often create a sense of urgency to get its organizations up to speed. Intel thus serves as a rallying point for change initiatives on several fronts.

Vadasz points to the development of a communications device that facilitated the commercial development of teleconferencing. Intel acted as project leader, but was one of thirteen makers of various components that worked together to deliver a total capability. In some cases, Intel invested in third-party firms to speed things along. Putting its money behind its ambitions is a classic aspect of Intel's change initiative. Another is the maintenance of market intelligence efforts that keep Intel in the know and allow it to adapt to market segment demands.

Even in the unlikely event that change would not be a challenge, Intel would not get too comfortable, because it is "always worried about the competition," Vadasz states. Yet, Intel enjoys competing, because a world without competition is not good for the customer and "is not good for us or for anybody else."

That attitude puts great responsibility on Intel's corporate business development group, which Intel works to the maximum. Vadasz describes the organization's mission as follows: "We try to understand the capabilities of the whole family of products in a market segment. We put in multiple teams to develop a broad range of product lines. At any given time, Intel works on three generations of microprocessors. We look not just at microprocessors but at the big picture. We take a top-down view of the market segment, even though we don't deliver all the elements to it. We try to understand what needs to be there. We often help other companies develop the technology and the capability to be there at the right time. In fact, we invest in many of these companies so that they can do their job."

Nothing less than that ambitious approach is required in view of what Intel is discovering about the vagaries of its current market segment, in which growth in PC use continues, while the Internet explodes in influence. But it's a struggle to adapt to the twin trends.

"Even without the stimulus from the Internet and other developments, sales of PCs were running at 60 million units in 1996 and should reach the 100 million mark by the end of the decade," Vadasz notes. But it is difficult to make firmer plans for capitalizing on this natural potential because the infrastructure needed to support the Internet is still awaiting full development. As a result, PC sales may eventually be held back because of the lack of high-bandwidth connections between the Internet and the home. As an alternative, Intel and other companies are developing "hybrid technologies" that mix low-bandwidth connections, such as telephone lines, with newer high-bandwidth ones, such as satellites and cable modems, to maximize the advantages of the Internet for the home PC user.

The drumbeat of change goes on as the challenges proliferate. It's when the technologies are most complex that the simplicity of deengineering is the shining star for the company that manages its own change initiatives.

# Paul Wahl
## SAP America Incorporated

In its seven years of existence SAP America Incorporated has enjoyed meteoric growth and continues to be a rising star in the software field. Results have been eye-popping, and SAP has plans to continue growing at an accelerated rate. Paul Wahl, SAP's chief executive, regards a total commitment to continual change as one of the firm's primary competitive weapons, and thinks that an ongoing emphasis on change-responsiveness will fortify SAP's competitive advantage in the future.

Wahl sketches the company's prospects in terms of a "react quickly or go under" scenario. He takes the view that in the software industry "business will never be the same." New products and new technologies, many with short life cycles, are constantly streaming into the marketplace, and major competitors vie ceaselessly for position and share.

That is not a setting in which an ambitious player can remain complacent when a change trigger hits. Rather, say change-responsive executives like Wahl, the survivors that show premier results will be those who proactively create and manage change.

SAP America, an outgrowth of a German company, is a specialist in client/server applications, one of the largest and fastest-growing sectors of the software field, with worldwide revenues already past the $2 billion-a-year mark. It currently has a 31% worldwide share of this market, much of it built by cutting into the positions enjoyed by older, sometimes larger, software companies.

Since 1992, sales have jumped from $40 million to $710 million, and the people side of the business has grown commensurately, with a 1,500-person work force now in place compared with just 100 five years earlier. The customer base, which numbered only twenty companies in 1992, has now exploded to more than 700.

SAP (an acronym for Systems Applications & Products) established its U.S. outpost at the urging of existing customers. That development was the result of industrial globalization – one of the great change triggers buffeting every known industry and market – and the need of large, geographically expanding corporations to find the right business tools, no matter where they expand. It also reinforced client confidence that SAP would be able to satisfy their requirements on a worldwide basis.

One major reason for this endorsement is that SAP constantly monitors the highly eclectic software/information systems market, spots the change triggers early, devises appropriate new products, and is well-geared to detect the inevitable change triggers of the future. Amid drastic and constant change, says Wahl, the key to doing well is to cut through all the trends and countertrends and focus on ways to serve the customer better – with the "right product, at the right time, at the right price." If SAP shies away from this commitment, Wahl asserts, it will lose out to a competitor. That commitment can mean going the extra mile in cementing partner-like relationships with customers. "Management of a software company must go directly to the customer and expend its energy in understanding customer needs," Wahl states. That calls for ratcheting up customer service, customer needs, and customer wants to the highest priority links in the "supply chain of information."

SAP has thus used the market-focus and customer services aspects of deengineering to draw a blueprint that has guided phenomenal growth, managed concurrent change challenges, and set the course for the future based on the company's own skills. While strategy, operations, and a change-responsive culture fall naturally from its overall plan, SAP goes to great lengths to ensure that all of its people are in a change-oriented mode.

In the area of strategy and operations, SAP is on top of the future consequences of current changes, and predicts enormous opportunities from them. Wahl expects computer resources to become cheaper and to induce more people to use them. By the year 2000, he anticipates a billion users of the Internet and says that, with the entry of less sophisticated users on-line, software companies "must keep it simple to access information."

The quest for easier-to-use software is but one facet of the overall plan to stay on top of customer service efforts. On the industry side, Wahl stresses sensitivity to changing business scenarios so that SAP will be able to produce the software that allows its customers to manage change with their information systems. With elements in the supply chain in a state of flux, information systems are now the key tools for maintaining balance. The customer's primary demand is to get what it needs as quickly as possible to meet the demands for change.

As the principal change agent in a change-oriented, people business, Wahl actively works to make sure that his enthusiasm for change is infectious. The change agent is encouraged and rewarded, and the change-oriented corps is considered the wellspring of ideas for powering SAP's growth and honing its competitive edge. He says software companies "need to encourage suggestions from proactive employees for new business ventures." "Proactive people must be encouraged to keep on generating new ideas, even if some ideas fail," he asserts. "The proactive company makes change happen. It identifies change and generates new solutions."

Thus, Wahl is behind the concept that a company should be able to unleash change triggers in the marketplace, while keeping it attuned to the changes of its own making under the rubric of Total Company Alignment. Wahl is able to drive this approach because he possesses a knowledge of the market, with the realization that change is inevitable, and the leadership skills to impress these realities on both employees and customers.

Wahl is prominent in the ranks of the modern change-minded executives who promote client alliances to weather change triggers. He notes that "software is a driver of change in client companies." As a result, SAP's full-scale, aggressive marketing program includes education in the use of the software to identify the benefits of change. "The customer's success," Wahl remarks, "is SAP's success."

# Change Manager's
## Reference Guide 1990 - 1997

_____

# Change Manager's
## Reference Guide 1990-1997

Argyris, Chris, *Overcoming Organizational Defenses: Facilitating Organizational Learning* (Boston: Allyn & Bacon, 1990).

Beer, Michael, Eisenstat, R.A., and Spector, B., "Why Change Programs Don't Produce Change," *Harvard Business Review*, November/December 1990, pp. 158-166.

Beer, Michael, Eisenstat, R.A., and Spector, B. *The Critical Path to Corporate Renewal* (Boston, MA: Harvard Business School Press, 1990).

Beer, Michael, Eisenstat, R.A, and Biggadike, R., "Developing an Organization Capable of Implementing and Reformulating Strategy" (Working paper, Harvard Business School, 1990).

Belasco, James A., *Teaching the Elephant to Dance: The Manager's Guide to Empowering Change* (New York, Penguin Books, 1990).

Bennett, A., "Downsizing Doesn't Necessarily Bring an Upswing in Corporate Profitability," *The Wall Street Journal*, June 6, 1991.

Berger, Lance A. Sikora, M. J., Berger, D.R., eds., *The Change Management Handbook* (Burr Ridge, IL: Business One Irwin, 1994). \*\*\*

Berger, Lance A., Goulliart, F.J., King, W.C., and Useem, M., "The Age of Alignment," *Directors & Boards,* vol. 16, no. 1, Fall 1991, pp.13-15, 18.

Bolles, Richard, *What Color Is Your Parachute?* (Berkeley: Ten Speed Press, updated annually). \*\*\*

Bolman, L.G. and Deal, T.E., *Reframing Organizations* (San Francisco: Jossey-Bass, 1991).

Bray, D.W., ed., *A Guide to Human Resources Practice* (New York: Guilford Press, 1991).

Bridges, William, *Managing Transitions* (Reading, MA: Addison-Wesley, 1991).

Burke, W. Warner and Litwin, G.H., "A Causal Model of Organizational Performance and Change," *Journal of Management*, vol.18, no. 3 (1992), pp. 523-545.

Burke, W. Warner, Spencer, Janet L., Clark, Lawrence P., and Coruzzi, Celeste, "Managers Get a 'C' in Managing Change," *Training and Development Journal*, May 1991.

Byrne, John A., "The Virtual Corporation," *Business Week*, February 8, 1993, pp. 98-103.

Carnavale, Anthony Patrick, *America and the New Economy* (San Francisco: Jossey-Bass, 1991).

Champy, James, *Reengineering Management* (New York: Harper Business, 1995).

Charan, R., "How Networks Reshape Organizations for Results," *Harvard Business Review*, September/October 1991, pp.104-115.

Coates, J.F., Jarrat, J., and Mahaffie, J., *Future Work* (San Francisco: Jossey-Bass, 1991).

Conner, D. R., *Managing at the Speed of Change* (New York: Villiard Books, 1993).

Csikszentmihalyi, Mihaly, *Flow: The Psychology of Optimal Experience* (New York: Harper & Row, 1990).

Dalton, Richard, "Lose the Sweatshop Mentality," *Information Week*, July 5, 1993, p. 63.

Drucker, Peter, *Managing for the Future* (New York: Penguin Books, 1992).

Drucker, Peter, "The New Society of Organizations," *Harvard Business Review*, September/October, 1992.

Drucker, Peter, *Post-Capitalist Society* (New York: Harper Business, 1993).

Duck, Jeanie Daniel, "Managing Change: The Art of Balancing," *Harvard Business Review*, vol. 71, no. 6, November/December 1993, pp. 109-118.

Fisher, S., "Cutting Costs or Re-Building Business?" *European Management Journal*, March 1993, pp. 74-79.

Fitz-enz, Jac, *How to Measure Human Resources Management* (New York: McGraw-Hill, 1995, 2nd ed.).

Fligstein, N., *Transformation of Corporate Control* (Cambridge, MA: Harvard University Press, 1990).

Garvin, David A., "Building a Learning Organization," *Harvard Business Review*, vol. 71, no. 4, July/August 1993, pp. 78-91.

Giblin, E. J., Wiegman, G.A., and Sanfilippo, F. "Bringing Pay Up to Date," *Personnel*, November 1990, pp. 17-18.

Glass, H., ed., *Handbook of Business Strategy* (Boston: Warren, Gorham & Lambert, 1991).

Goodstein, L.D. and Burke, W.W., "Creating Successful Organizational Change," *Organizational Dynamics*, vol. 19, no. 4 (1991), pp. 5-17.

Goss, Tracy, Pascale, Richard, and Athos, Anthony, "The Reinvention Rollercoaster: Risking the Present for a Powerful Future," *Harvard Business Review*, vol. 71, no. 6, November/December 1993, pg. 98.

Gould, Lawrence, "What About the Worker Who Doesn't Want to Be Empowered?" *Managing Automation*, September 1993.

Greenwood, Royston and Hinings, C.R., "Understanding Strategic Change: The Contributions of Archetypes," *Academy of Management Journal*, vol. 36, no. 5, October 1993, pp. 1,052-1,081.

Hakim, Cliff, *We Are All Self-Employed* (San Francisco: Berrett-Koehler Publishers, 1994). ***

Hall, B.H., "The Impact of Corporate Structuring in Industrial Research and Development," *Brookings Papers on Economic Activity: Microeconomics* (Washington, DC: Brookings Institution, 1990).

Hammer, Michael, "Reengineering Work: Don't Automate, Obliterate," *Harvard Business Review*, vol. 68, no. 4, July/August 1990, pp. 104-112.

Hammer, Michael and Champy, James, *Reengineering the Corporation: A Manifesto for Business Revolution* (New York: Harper Business, 1993).

Howard, R., "The CEO as Organizational Architect: An Interview With Paul Allair," *Harvard Business Review*, September/October 1992.

Jamieson, David and O'Mara, Julie, *Managing Workforce 2000: Gaining the Diversity Advantage* (San Francisco: Jossey-Bass, 1991).

Jensen, M.C. and Murphy, K.J., "CEO Incentives – It's Not How Much You Pay, But How," *Harvard Business Review*, May/June 1990, pp. 138-153.

Porter, A., "The Ten Commandments of Skill-Based Pay," *Journal of Compensation and Benefits*, March/April 1991, pp. 44-47.

Kanter, R.M., *The Challenge of Organizational Change: How Companies Experience It and Leaders Guide It* (New York: Free Press, 1992).

Kim, Daniel H., "The Link Between Individual and Organizational Learning," *Sloan Management Review*, vol. 35, no. 1, Fall 1993, pp. 37-50.

Kissler, Gary D., *The Change Riders: Managing the Power of Change* (Reading, MA: Addison-Wesley, 1991).

Kochan, Thomas A. and Useem, Michael, eds., *Transforming Organizations* (New York: Oxford University Press, 1992).

Kotter, J.P. *A Force for Change* (New York: Free Press, 1990).

Kotter, J.P. and Heskett, J.L., *Corporate Culture and Performance* (New York: Free Press, 1992).

Krieg, Richard M., "The New Era: Workers as Assets," *Chicago Tribune*, July 23, 1993, Section 11, pp. 15ff.

Kuchel, Gerald, *Reaching the Peak Performance Zone* (New York: Amacom, 1994).

Lawler, Edward E. III, *Strategic Pay* (San Francisco: Jossey-Bass, 1990).

Lawler, Edward E. III, *The Ultimate Advantage: Creating the High-Involvement Organization* (San Francisco: Jossey-Bass, 1992).

Leonard-Barton, Dorothy, "The Factory as a Learning Laboratory," *Sloan Management Review*, vol. 34, no.1, Fall 1992, pp. 23-38.

Loden, Marilyn and Rosener, Judy B., *Workforce America!: Managing Employee Diversity as a Vital Resource* (Homewood, IL: Business One Irwin, 1991).

Martin, Peter, "Changing the Mind of the Corporation," *Harvard Business Review*, vol. 71, no. 6, November/December 1993, pp. 81-94.

Miller, Danny, "The Architecture of Simplicity," *Academy of Management Review*, vol. 18, no. 1, January 1993, pp. 116-138.

Miller, William, "A New Perspective for Tomorrow's Workforce," *Industry Week*, May 6, 1991, pp. 6-11.

Mills, Daniel Quinn and Friesen, Bruce, "The Learning Organization," *European Management Journal*, June 1992, pp. 146-156.

Mintzberg, Henry, *The Rise and Fall of Strategic Planning: Reconceiving Roles for Planning, Plans, Planners* (New York: Free Press, 1994).

Moad, Jeff, "Does Reengineering Really Work?" *Datamation*, August 1, 1993, pp. 22 ff.

Mohrman, M. Jr., Mohrman, S.A., Ledford, G.E. Jr., Cummings, T.G., and Lawler, E.E., *Large Scale Organizational Change* (San Francisco: Jossey-Bass, 1991).

Morton, M.S. Scott, ed., *The Corporation of the 1990s* (New York: Oxford University Press, 1991).

Nadler, David A., *Organizational Architecture* (San Francisco: Jossey-Bass, 1992).

Neil, Terence V., "The Board as Change Masters," *Directors & Boards*, vol. 18, no. 3, Spring 1994, pp. 55-56.

Nickel, J.E. and O'Neal, S., "Small-Group Incentives: Gain Sharing in the

Microcosm," *Compensation and Benefits Review*, March/April 1991, pp. 44-47.

Noer, David M., *Healing the Wounds: Overcoming the Trauma of Layoffs and Revitalizing Downsized Organizations* (San Francisco: Jossey-Bass, 1993).

Osburn, J.D., et al., *Self-Directed Work Teams* (Homewood, IL: Business One Irwin, 1990).

Ostroff, F. and Smith, D., "The Horizontal Organization," *The McKinsey Quarterly*, 1992, pp. 148-168.

Pennings, J.M., "Strategic Reward Systems: A Cross-National Comparison," *Journal of Management Studies,* vol. 23, March 1993.

Pepper, Jon, "The Horizontal Organization," *Information Week*, August 17, 1992, pp. 32ff.

Pettigrew, A. and Whipp, R., *Managing Change for Competitive Success* (Oxford, England: Blackwell Publishers Ltd., 1991).

Potter, Wendy, "The Stages of Change: A Theory and Model of the Process of Organizational Change" (unpublished paper, People Tech, 1993).

Powell, Reed M., "A Point of View: Doing More With Less," *National Productivity Review*, Winter 1990, p. 1.

Prahalad, C.K. and Hamel, Gary, "The Core Competence of the Corporation," *Harvard Business Review*, vol. 68, no. 3, May/June 1990, pp. 79-91.

Prochaska, James O., DiClemente, Carlo C., and Norcross, John C., "In Search of How People Change: Applications to Addictive Behaviors," *American Psychology*, vol. 47, no. 9, September 1992, pp. 1,102-1,114.

Quinn, James B., *Intelligent Enterprise* (New York: Free Press, 1992).

Quinn, James B. and Paquette, P.C., "Technology and Services: Creating Organization Revolutions," *Sloan Management Review*, vol. 31, no. 2, Winter 1990, pp.67-78.

Reich, Robert, *The Work of Nations: Preparing Ourselves for 21st Century Capitalism* (New York: Alfred A. Knoff, 1991).

Rock, M.L. and Berger, Lance A., eds., *The Compensation Handbook* (New York: McGraw-Hill, 1991, 3rd. ed.).

Sanfilippo, F., Wiegman, G.A., and Giblin, E.J., "A Compensation Strategy for the 1990s," *The Human Resource Professional*, Fall 1991, pp. 47-51.

Schaffer, R. and Thomson, R.A., "Successful Change Programs Begin With Results," *Harvard Business Review*, January/February 1992, pp. 80-89.

Scheiner, C.E., Shaw, D.G., and Beatty, R.W, "Companies' Attempts to Improve Performance While Containing Costs: Quick Fix Versus Lasting Change," *Human Resource Planning*, vol.15, no. 3, 1992, pp. 1-25.

Scheiner, C.E., Shaw, D.G., and Beatty, R.W., "Performance Measurement and Management: A Tool for Strategy Execution," *Human Resource Management*, vol. 30, no. 3 ,1991, pp. 279-301.

Schrange, M., *Shared Minds: The New Technologies of Collaboration* (New York: Random House, 1990).

Senge, Peter, *The Fifth Discipline: The Art and Practice of the Learning Organization* (New York: Doubleday, 1990).

Shapiro, Eileen, *Fad Surfing in the Boardroom* (Reading, MA: Addison-Wesley, 1995). ***

Smye, Marti with McKague, Anne, *You Don't Change a Company by Memo* (Toronto: Key Porter Books, 1994).

Spencer, L. and Spencer, S., *Competence at Work* (New York: Wiley-Interscience, 1993).

Stacey, R.D., *Managing the Unknowable* (San Francisco: Jossey-Bass, 1992).

Stalk, G., Evans, P., and Shulman, L., "Competing on Capabilities: The New Rules of Corporate Strategy," *Harvard Business Review*, vol. 69, no. 2, 1992, pp. 57-69.

Stewart, Thomas A., "Reengineering: The Hot New Managing Tool," *Fortune*, August 23, 1993, pp. 44ff.

Tofler, A., *Power Shift* (New York: Bantam, 1990).

Tracey, W., ed., *Human Resources Management and Development Handbook* (New York: American Management Association, 1993).

Ulrich, D. and Lake, D., *Organizational Capability* (New York: Wiley, 1990).

Ulrich, D., "Strategic and Human Resource Planning: Linking Customers and Employees," *Human Resource Planning*, vol. 15, no. 2, 1992, pp. 47-62.

Veneklasen, W.D. and Cornell, P.T., *The Human Component in the Healthy Office* (Grand Rapids, MI: Steelcase Inc., 1991).

Vroom, Victor H., *Some Personality Determinants of the Effects of Participation* (Englewood, NJ: Prentice-Hall, 1960).

Walker, J.W., *Human Resource Planning* (New York: McGraw-Hill, 1992).

Winslow, Charles D. and Bramer, William L., *Future Work: Putting Knowledge to Work in the Knowledge Economy* (New York: Free Press, 1994).

Womack, J., Jones, J.T., and Roos, D., *The Machine That Changed the World: The Story of Lean Production* (New York: Harper Collins, 1990).

Woodward, Harry, *Navigating Through Change* (Burr Ridge, IL: Business One Irwin, 1994).

Wright, L., and Smye, Marti, *Corporate Abuse* (New York: MacMillan, 1996)

Zaleznik, Abraham, "Managers and Leaders: Are They Different?", *Harvard Business Review*, vol. 70, no. 2, March/April 1992, pp. 126-135.

*** Cited in the book

# Index

# Index